MINIATURE GARDENS

Sheila Howarth

Marshall Cavendish London & New York

Facing title page: Vriesea fenestralis is a member of a species which originated in South America, and would be the perfect centrepiece for a terrarium or Wardian case. Title page: A concrete container, durable and weatherproof, is planted with a palm and colourful, trailing nasturtiums. This page: A miniature kitchen garden grown in pots in a balcony or backyard can yield a surprising amount of produce.

Published by Marshall Cavendish
Publications Limited
58 Old Compton Street
London W1V 5PA

© Marshall Cavendish Limited 1977

First printed 1977

Printed in Great Britain by
Redwood Burn Limited
Trowbridge & Esher

ISBN 0 85685 246 5 (hardback)
      0 85685 257 0 (softback)

CONTENTS

SMALL SCALE
GARDENING

*No matter where you live or what kind
of life-style you prefer there is room for
growing plants and flowers indoors or out.
Above: An apartment kitchen window
accommodates herbs, bulbs and flowering
houseplants. Left: If you have a
conservatory or sun room there is no end
to the number of ways you can 'garden'
on a small scale.*

AS GARDENS SHRINK to make way for wider roads, and others sink completely into the foundations of tower blocks and housing estates, plant lovers are devising ingenious ways of keeping in touch with nature. This, happily, can bring them in even closer touch with growing plants than in large gardens.

This book uses the term 'miniature gardens' in its wider sense, meaning small scale, rather than something which, to be appreciated, must be seen through a magnifying glass! It suggests how to create a garden in a limited area, whether there is open soil, or there is none; mostly using collections of plants to create a natural effect, rather than a series of individual plants in a collection of assorted pots.

There is enormous scope for anyone with an inventive mind and a will to get their own way with plants which often have a reputation for being 'difficult'.

This is often achieved by proper distrust of 'expert' advice. We hope the many ideas in this book will stimulate imagination, and persuade you to experiment.

There is no place in any living area—house, flat, caravan or even tent—where some plant cannot be grown either inside or out—to look at, to smell, to decorate, to eat—or a combination of all or several of these.

Indoors, windowsills are the most usual locations for small individual pots or dish gardens, which can be moved from one aspect to another, as the weather or their growing moods change. Many indoor plants are at their happiest in the bathroom or kitchen, but without exception they detest draughts. There is tremendous satisfaction in seeing a plant rallying round from what appeared to be its death bed, when you have eventually found the position and treatment it really needs.

Specially designed containers can be bought to fit almost any awkward area

Small scale gardening can simply mean easily maintained pots or tubs in the garden or patio. Below: Lilies, pelargoniums, ferns and bamboo crowd together in the corner of an otherwise 'flowerless' garden. Below right: Splashes of colour in spring and early summer can be confined to tubs or concrete containers.

of a house such as a window recess, and there are many unusual or space-saving containers to choose from, ranging from bottle gardens, illuminated indoor terraria to hanging containers for trailing plants.

Window boxes usually give the most pleasure and scope for the flat or town dweller. They are at a comfortable height to look after, and can be planned to be seen from whichever aspect you please, whether sitting or standing, or from below.

Hanging baskets can swing around the front porch or be attached to walls; but more easily reached containers are the greatest boon for restricted gardens. They come in all sizes, weights, shapes,

Some more of the many versions of miniaturized gardening which are open to the keen amateur.
Left: A sink, or trough, garden is the perfect location for hardy, cushion-forming alpines, evergreens and small succulents. Below left: An indoor dish garden of house plants, using variegated foliage for colour and textural effect.

materials, and can be put at any height to suit your viewing eye, or your aching back.

A distinct advantage of container gardening is that you are not limited to a particular type of soil. Experiment with mixtures until you find just the one demanded by particularly fussy plants, such as those requiring an acid soil. Whatever you grow can be permanent or seasonal, trouble-free or demanding. You are the one to make and break the rules. The joy of small-scale gardening is that no permanent damage can be done. You cannot poison a 200-year-old oak, or a 30-year-old asparagus bed. Any dead plants can quickly be removed and replaced, and any change of mind about the attractions of what you are growing will not cost the earth, as it were, to change.

The advantages of confined gardening are tremendous. There are no bare patches, all the earth space is planted.

Very little maintenance is required— just occasional dead-heading, replacing, a little weeding and feeding, and a careful eye to watering. Disabled and stiff-jointed people can cope with their gardens quite independently and even grow their own salads and herbs if they like them.

Town children can have their own sink garden, for the odd broad bean plant, a few radishes or even an ambitious runner bean. No expensive tools are needed at all, just a discarded knife, fork and spoon from the kitchen of a size to suit your purpose, or a small trowel and handfork, and a small watering can with a fine rose.

Miniature or small-scale gardens are not confined to pots or containers. They can be gardens within gardens, which though restricted, can still produce a great variety of fruit and vegetables, using methods and varieties we suggest.

Whatever your garden, in or out, it

Above: Sink gardens and tubs make interesting edgings to a raised lawn. Right: A strawberry barrel yields masses of fruit in a very confined space. Opposite: Bottle gardens are easier to prepare than many people think and they require very little maintenance. Instructions for planting and care are on page 56.

8

can be completely individual, with you the complete master of it . . . whether Japanese in style, formal, informal, vegetable, balcony or hanging. It can give enormous satisfaction all the year round, with the minimum outlay and attention, and the maximum enjoyment and visual appeal.

SINK
GARDENS

*When talking about miniature gardens,
most people probably think of sink or
trough gardens. These tiny environments
are usually turned into rock gardens or
alpine collections. They are easy to
maintain and ideal for the disabled.*

MINIATURE GARDENING can be at its most articulate and specialized when confined to a sink. Because of its manageable size and height you can give it the extra care which some alpines need if you are going to produce a dwarf replica rock garden. Or it can be a playground for plants which refuse to grow in anything but a lime soil, or others which thrive only on an acid, peaty one. In a confined space you can give your treasured choices just the treatment they need, and with several sink gardens, you can have a great variety of 'fussy' plants, each dining at separate tables, as it were, and each with a character entirely its own, all the year round. If you refer to the plant list at the back of this book you will find some of the plants which like special conditions, such as the ericas (heather) or aubrieta, which thrives on lime.

Sinks are ideal for shallow-rooted plants which like their heads in the sun and their roots groping around in cool, well-drained, stony soil.

Containers

The actual sinks you use will depend on your taste, your pocket and your ingenuity. The Portland sinks of more than a century ago, which were quarried in great numbers and were used under pumps and as animal water troughs, as well as in the house, are now scarce and extremely expensive. At first, as they were discarded and replaced by enamel sinks, then stainless steel and plastic, they could be had for the asking. But now, country people know that a stone trough is not just junk, and that it will fetch a high price in an antique shop.

Other sinks can be bought made of cement or tufa rock which has a rough texture and blends well in a garden setting. However, the least expensive and most satisfying way of acquiring a sink is by making it yourself, either from scratch, or by disguising a thrown-out white glazed sink. Some people even use these without disguising them, although it is difficult to see the attraction!

Most original sinks can be created using broken pieces of paving stone, walling stone, broken pieces of marble, broken or whole decorative tiles as mosaic, or even flint stones. Choose what will fit in most happily with the setting you want for the sink. Coloured tiles and marble for instance would look their best in a formal, paved area or by a swimming pool.

Demolition yards and builders merchants are the places to search for what you want. Flints can be scavenged in all sorts of shapes, or bought in regular sizes as a side product of sand pits.

Use a bottomless wooden box or frame a few inches higher than the eventual depth of the sink; this allows for the depth of the base. Make a 5cm (2in) concrete base, putting in plugs of wood, metal, cork etc, which can be knocked out when the cement has set, to provide drainage holes. Using mortar, build up whatever materials you have chosen on the inside, keeping straight edges and the coloured sides of tiles against the wooden sides. The walls should be at least 2cm (1in) thick, but, depending on what is used, not so heavy that the sink cannot be lifted when it has dried out!

There are a variety of techniques for 'ageing' glazed sinks, so they become passable replicas of the old, quarried stone sinks. First, cut away any plumbing remains round the drainage hole underneath, so the sink can stand level. The metal fitment can usually be un-

Below: Constructing a 'sink' from concrete, using a bottomless wooden box as a frame.

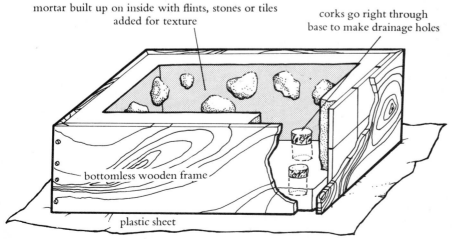

mortar built up on inside with flints, stones or tiles added for texture

corks go right through base to make drainage holes

bottomless wooden frame

plastic sheet

Above: At the Royal Horticultural Society's gardens at Wisley, outside London, there is a splendid collection of trough gardens, each one planted up in an individual way with succulents and miniature conifers. The trough on the left contains species of erica and saxifraga, on the right a selection of houseleeks.

screwed and a hammer and chisel will deal with anything which remains.

Thoroughly scrub the sink outside with detergent and water to get rid of any grease, and let it dry. For the coating, mix two parts peat and one part each of sharp sand and cement with just enough water to bind them together. If you make the mixture too wet you will not be able to mould it properly to the sink. Before this can be attempted, use an old paintbrush to cover the outside of the sink and 7 to 10cm (3 to 4in) from the top inside with a thick layer of adhesive. When this starts to become tacky, press the mixture into it about 1cm ($\frac{1}{2}$in) thick. This can be done with your hands or a trowel.

Though these are the general instructions, much depends on the type of adhesive used. Follow the manufacturer's instructions. Be generous with the adhesive, or the coating will fall away and leave bald patches of porcelain. A 10 litre (2 gallon) bucket full of the mixture is usually enough to cover a normal sized sink. The overcoat

should be allowed to dry out slowly under a cover of sacking or plastic. Damp it occasionally with a sprinkle of water, for the longer it takes to set, the better. Do not start to fill it with plants for at least two weeks.

This mixture and method gives a rough, 'old stone' finish which looks even better as it weathers and begins to turn green. Some people prefer a more 'pasty' mix using equal parts of cement and peat to three parts of sharp sand, applied to the drying-off adhesive a little at a time. You can leave the finish as smooth or rough as you please.

Another way of putting a stone finish on a glazed sink is to encase it in fine wire mesh netting outside, and a few inches down the inside. Press into this a mixture of four parts sand to one of cement. Just before this is quite set and hard, score the surface fairly deeply with slanting, irregular lines. Wet the surface and put on a final thin rendering of the usual mixture of two parts peat to one part each of sand and cement. This gives the appearance of York stone.

Drainage and position

Whatever type of sink you use, drainage is essential. There must be at least one escape route. In the case of old, or glazed, sinks there is usually just one at one end, and when in position, the sink has only to be tilted slightly in that direction. The drainage hole or holes must be prevented from being blocked by covering them with perforated zinc, broken tiles or slate.

When old sinks, usually the shallow ones, have no drainage hole and there is the risk of the whole thing disintegrating if holes are bored, it is better not to try. Use extra drainage material at the bottom and choose plants which need little moisture. A soilless potting compost is also a good idea as it is very absorbent.

Get the sink into position before starting to put anything inside, as it will be too heavy to manoeuvre once it is filled. Sinks can balance on central plinths, or supports at each end of brick, ornamental stone, old chimney stacks or anything which fits your purpose. They are easier to look after if raised a few feet from the ground. This also allows a good circulation of air and shows off the plants to best advantage. Sinks can be placed flat on low walls, or on the edge of ponds, but run the risk of pests invading them more easily as well as being at the mercy of cats and dogs.

Where you put the sink depends entirely on why you wanted one in the first place; as a colourful ornament in a soilless area; to grow rock plants without having to get on hands and knees to look after them; or to grow a special family of plants which will only thrive in a particular soil and position. In general, an open, sunny position is best for sink gardens of all types.

Planting a sink garden

When drainage and position have been assured, filling can start. There must be at least 2cm (1in) of broken crocks, pebbles or rubble at the bottom, followed by a layer of moist peat, or decayed compost, then filled almost to the top with soil. This can be a mixture of

Below: Planting a sink garden. Bottom left: A sink garden of flowering plants can brighten a dull exterior wall. Bottom right: Petunias and French marigolds in a sink garden raised to waist height on brick pillars.

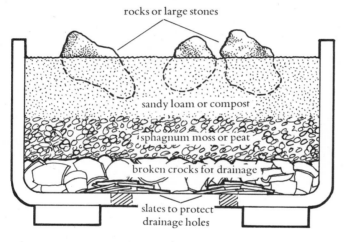

rocks or large stones

sandy loam or compost

sphagnum moss or peat

broken crocks for drainage

slates to protect drainage holes

equal parts of good loam, peat and leaf mould, with a generous amount of gritty sand scattered into it; or an ordinary, proprietary potting compost. A light, fertile soil straight from the garden is quite adequate, unless the sink is intended for specimens with special needs.

For a permanent miniature rock garden effect, partly bury a few carefully chosen pieces of stone, tilted to resemble a natural rock stratum. This not only improves the appearance, but provides a cool root run for plants which need it, such as alpines.

Give the sink contents a good soaking and allow it to settle for a few days before planting. When planting is finished, press the soil around the roots and add more soil to fill any depressions. Finally you may like to cover exposed soil with a layer of chippings, if possible of the same material as the protruding stones. Otherwise, use limestone, granite or washed gravel. This gives an overall 'rocky' look as well as keeping the plants clean and preventing the soil from drying out. It also deters weed seeds from germinating. However, be careful not to use limestone chippings among plants which demand an acid soil.

Make sure the new garden does not go short of water through spring and summer, and when it needs water, do the job thoroughly, with a rose on the watering can to avoid disturbing the plants.

If it is to be a miniature rock garden, put dwarf conifers in first, perhaps two or three of different shapes and colour —pointed or bushy; green, golden or blue. Then put trailing plants around the sides, which will spill over the edges to soften the hard lines of the sink and give it an air of maturity. Among the protruding rocks add tiny rosette-forming rock plants, which will hug the surface, but never become rampant and make a nuisance of themselves. Do not be tempted to cram in too many occupants at the first planting. Be content to look at more rock chippings than plants, until they establish themselves and

spread out. Overcrowding at the start will only lead to disappointment as some of the plants will be unable to thrive.

Plants to include in this kind of sink are the sedums (stonecrops), sempervivums (houseleeks), and saxifrages (rockfoils). Any one of these families, with their infinite variety, could fill an entire sink on its own.

Of the dwarf conifers, which should not grow more than about one centimetre ($\frac{1}{2}$in) a year, look at *Chamaecyparis obtusa nana, Cryptomeria pygmea, Juniperis communis compressa, Picea albertiana concia, Thuya plicata rogersii.*

Shrubby plants to include are *Genista delphinensis* and *G. sylvestris, Hypericum reptans,* dwarf species of hebe, lavender *L. spica* 'Baby Blue', *Cytisus Ardoinii* (broom), and *Daphne arbuscula. Salix arbuscula* is another interesting species, a willow which grows to only about 23cm (9in).

Other plants which take kindly to

One of the many delightful cushion-forming plants which are ideal for sink gardens, Dionysia curviflora comes from Persia and flowers in spring.

restricted conditions include aethionema (Lebanon candytuft); *Antennaria dioica rosea*, a silver leaved creeper; *Aspersula lilaciflora*; *Androsace sarmentosa*; *Armeria caespitosa* (pink flowered thrift); *Campanula arvetica* and *C. cochlearifolia*; *Dianthus alpinus*; *Erinus alpinus*; *Phlox douglasii*, with white and pale blue flowers; *Iris lacustris*; *Primula farinosa*, which has pink flowers; *Lewisia howellii* (bitter-wort); *Micromeria corsica*; *Mentha requienii*; *Potentilla aurea plena*; *Rosa roukettii*; *Saponaria caespitosa*; *Saxifraga cotyledon*, which has delightful silver rosettes with white flowers; saxifrages of the Kabschia species, carpeters with white and pink flowers; and *Sedum spathulifolium*, a purple-leaved carpeter. Others for which you might like to find space are tiny ferns, mosses, miniature violas with wonderfully varied faces, and dwarf penstemons. See first what garden centres have to offer and then visit specialist nurseries or send for their catalogues.

Seasonal plantings

You may prefer to use your sink for a less permanent collection, or have several sinks for different seasons and species. They can be used in much the same way as window boxes. Fill them with unusual dwarf bulbs for the winter and spring, such as dainty species of crocus, dwarf tulips, tiny bulbous iris; *Scilla siberica* and the snowdrops; triteleia, *Leucoium vernum*, tiny narcissi; and some of the less familiar grape hyacinths, which are easy to grow. There are white ones as well as all shades of blue, some double, others feathered.

The bulbs can be lifted out when they become unsightly and left to die down naturally in a shallow trench in the garden, or a pot or box, and be dried off for use the following autumn.

The sink can then take on a new look with any summer plants you fancy—trailers, half-hardy shrubs, annuals, foliage plants, or a mixture of everything. As these fade away they can be replaced with small asters, French marigolds and chrysanthemums which can continue into the autumn, when the bulbs are ready to go back again. A few perennial evergreen trailers, such as ivies, can be kept in pots as reserves, and planted with the bulbs, so that the sink does not look completely naked while you are waiting for the bulbs to come up.

Sinks look delightful planted with miniature roses of a single colour, and if you have several, they can each be in complimentary tones. They make a trouble-free permanent planting if you add a few evergreen creepers which enjoy the same soil, slightly on the limey side.

Maintaining a sink garden

Looking after sink gardens cannot possibly be described as a task or job. Sinks containing permanent plants need very little attention, apart from watering in dry weather, removing any weed seeds and dead flower heads, and an occasional reviver with a liquid fertilizer, appropriate to the particular plants and used strictly according to the manufacturer's instructions.

When annual plants are grown in sinks, the soil will have to be renewed annually, but there is no need to go right down to the drainage material.

Sinks which are not used as alpine gardens and do not have the soil covered with chipping can be fed with slow acting fertilizers such as bone meal. Annuals will need to be dead-headed frequently, and mixed plantings must be watched carefully so that anything in a poor state of health can be removed at once, and replaced, when you have made sure the illness is not due to the state of the soil. It is more likely to be due to under- or over-watering.

Divide any plants which outstrip their space, by putting in a small handfork, holding the main plant down with one hand, and dragging off the excess growth. This can be the start of yet another sink.

Below: A visit to a good nursery, or, shown here, the Alpine House at the RHS garden, will give you an idea of the range of plants suitable for sink gardens.

WINDOW BOXES, TUBS, BARRELS, POTS

*Plants that prefer to grow in the open air
are generally much less temperamental
than house plants, so a window box, tub
or other container is a trouble-free way
of growing them in limited space.*

The choice of containers is almost limitless. Here an old wicker basket (right), raised on bricks, is put into service as a container for alyssum, lobelia, marigolds and pelargoniums, while (below) an old pottery bread crock makes an attractive container for daffodils.

Gardening in pots and containers has become both a cult and a necessity. More and more people are living in apartments or have gardens so small that plants have to be confined. In addition, plants which grow in the open air are rarely temperamental, so window boxes or tubs are easy to maintain.

The main problem when embarking on this easy-going form of gardening is that there are too many containers to choose from. The good old earthy clay pot is still with us but has been superceded by other, lighter materials, and improvisation has brought on a rash of extraordinary containers from old tyres, wheelbarrows, tin cans and old leather boots, to chamber pots, leaking wooden dinghies, chimney pots and ornate baths. Demolition yards are the most inspiring sources of unusual containers if you can keep your head and remember the setting for which they are intended.

With more conventional containers there is a wide diversity of design, from the humble flower pot to the sophisticated, automatically watered plant trough. Materials range in age and type from the old stone trough to the very latest plastic. These include asbestos, cement, clay, metal, fibreglass and wood, and can be adapted for both outdoor and indoor use depending on the appearance and strength.

Some manufacturers use extruded polystyrene to produce very light and attractive containers with speckled or marbled tone finish. A considerable advantage of this type is that they quickly absorb warmth which keeps the compost in them much more comfortable than that in stone or clay ones. The plants stay evenly warm and retain moisture for some time. As the material is smooth, the containers will not scratch outdoor tiles or paving, or indoor furniture. Finally, they are weatherproof.

Choice of design

Many tubs, tanks, urns and vases made of fibreglass are based on classic designs and given a lead finish. They are perfect copies taken from the original moulds of the eighteenth century lead containers. Only by handling an empty one can you be sure whether it is ancient or modern—the latter have the great advantage of being featherweight. They are not cheap by modern standards, but are strong, easily cleaned and frost-proof and look well beside old brick and weathered colour-wash walls.

The majority of nurserymen now use plastic pots because they are lighter, easy to scrub and pack, almost un-breakable, and plants in them dry out less quickly than those in clay, and so need less watering. On the reverse side they have little warmth in either appearance or behaviour. They seem to be strangely apart and out of sympathy with their contents, and if you have a lapse in your watering routine, they are quite unforgiving. However, it is possible to save the life of a plant, obviously on its last legs in a plastic pot, by transferring it to a clay one of the same size. When planting into new clay pots, they must be soaked for at least a day, so they will not sneak the moisture from the soil and leave the plants thirsty.

An unglazed clay pot is porous and lets air and moisture get in and out from both sides, which is a great help for the roots. Adversely this means that there is a great deal of condensation and you must water generously and more often.

There is much to commend the use of concrete and asbestos containers and there are several attractive designs available. The low flat bowls used in many public places look particularly effective in city back yards which have been completely paved. Either flat on the ground or raised on metal supports, their wide surface holds enough plants to make a really striking display.

For most purposes, wood is the

Below: The advantage of container gardening is splendidly illustrated here. This tiny city backyard has been transformed into a riot of summer colour with fuchsias, begonias, petunias, roses and pelargoniums, as well as smaller plants such as lobelia and 'Busy Lizzie'.
Right top: A more formal patio uses concrete containers with mainly foliage plants for effect.
Right below: An old wheel barrow painted in gay colours is planted with hyacinths.

natural choice, and the most sensible for a sunny position. The evaporation is much slower than in an earthenware container. They need drainage holes and should be treated inside with a safe bituminous paint—never creosote. All shapes and sizes can be bought or made, but half wine or beer casks are particularly attractive in a wide variety of situations.

The most useful sizes are 50cm (20in) across by 45cm (18in) high and 40cm (16in) across by 25cm (14in) high. These are usually sold in their natural colour which can be smartened up to suit their

background. They look very effective with the wood stained almost black and the iron bands painted white, or *vice versa*. The wood painted blue and the bands white, gives a refreshing look in the right setting, and deep shades of purple and rose have daring sophistication. It really depends what you intend to plant, and whether you want the container to feature in your overall scheme or to fade into insignificance.

Self-watering pots

Watering plants in pots or containers can be a problem, for instance, when

you go away on holiday, but this can be overcome by using automatically watered containers. A special range of attractive, high grade polystyrene pots and troughs are available, which keep plants continuously watered by means of a simple capillary system. Each has its own water-filling funnel and a visible individual water-level indicator. An advantage of this method is that individual plants can take up as much or little water as they want.

A standard trough measures 57cm (22½in) long by 18cm (7in) wide with an inside soil depth of 10cm (4in)—a larger trough measuring 64cm by 23cm (26½in by 9in) allows for a soil depth of 16cm (6½in). Self-watering pots range in size from 14cm (5½in) to 39cm (15½in) high: there are many designs, varying in shape, size, colour and finish. The system of watering usually consists of a water reservoir in the double wall of the pot, which supplies water to a wick or series of special wicks in the base. The wick is so arranged that it is in contact with the base of the soil in the pot. This ensures a constant supply of moisture which in turn is absorbed by the soil and taken up by the plant roots.

Wrought iron bases or stands are made in a variety of designs for automatically watered pots and troughs, and there is also a special wall support for some of the troughs. The metal stand supporting the plant containers, whether pots or troughs, sometimes takes the form of scrollwork, often covered in white polythene, both to make it more attractive and more weatherproof.

Below: A self-watering pot.

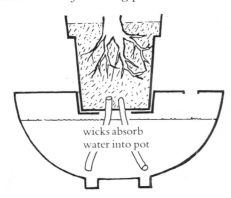

wicks absorb
water into pot

Choosing a window box

Window boxes can be a fascinating hobby for anyone with a windowsill not less than 15cm (6in) wide. It can be enjoyed even by those with aches and pains for whom bending and digging is out of the question. But there are two important points to bear in mind—that your lease does not forbid it, and that the boxes are absolutely safely fastened.

A box should be tailored to fit the space available as closely as possible. It must be at least 15cm (6in) wide and deep. Where possible it should have short legs or be raised on blocks of wood so that air can circulate beneath, and if your window is above ground floor level, it should be fitted with a tray underneath to make sure that excess water will not splatter anything below, particularly people.

Ready-made window boxes can be bought made of wood, galvanized iron, aluminium, plastic and fibreglass. Many of them have galvanized containers which can be planted and then just dropped into position, which makes it easy to keep up a virtual conveyor-belt supply of flowering containers. Plant up the spare containers before those on display in the window boxes are past their best, so that they are given a chance to settle. Keep them in a light place but out of fierce sun until the ones displayed start to tire, then replace them. The containers can also be used in the permanent window boxes filled with pot plants, which can be easily changed at will. They need much less attention if damp peat is packed around the pots.

A made-to-measure window box of teak, oak or cedar will inevitably look better than an ill-fitting affair made of artificial materials. Hardwoods look better unpainted and may either be oiled or varnished. Softwoods should be treated with preservative and can be painted or left natural.

The timber should be at least 1·3cm (½in) thick and the inside depth from 18cm (7in) to 25cm (10in). If the window sill exceeds 1½m (5ft) you may find it more convenient to make two boxes, each half the length, to make

Far left and left: Some of the
many different effects which can be
made with varied plantings in
window boxes. Below left:
Constructing a window box. The
best wood to use is prepared soft
wood 250mm × 25mm or 300mm
× 25mm (10in × 1in or 12in ×
1in). Either of these widths makes
a good height for the box, allowing
room for plenty of drainage
material under the soil, and at the
same time giving the roots of the
plants sufficient airing. The length
and width of the box should be
calculated according to the size of
the window sill, or the available
space. The diagram shows the
front and back pieces, the sides and
the base. To make a good-looking
job of the window box, make sure
you fit the sides and the base
inside the front and the back, so
that the end grain of the wood
used to make the sides and the base
does not show in front.
Drill two rows of 13mm (½in)
diameter holes for drainage at
100–125mm (4–5in) intervals in
the base. Glue and screw the
pieces together, using brass screws
and a waterproof glue.
Finish the top of the box with a
capping of 19mm (¾in) half-
round moulding or flat strips of
hardwood. This is the only
difficult part of the construction,
because the ends have to be mitred.
Finally, pin and glue the moulding
carefully to the box.

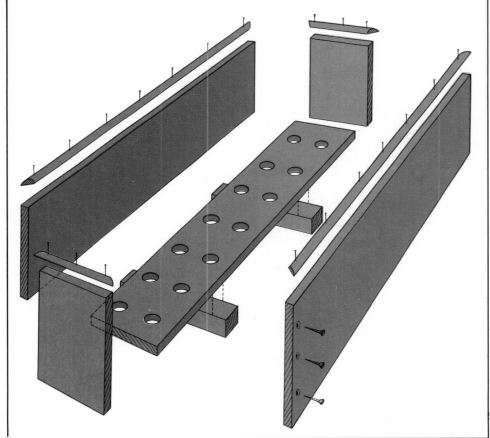

fixing and handling easier. If the front
of the box slopes at a slight angle out-
wards, it will be easier to grow trailing
plants in the box. It is best to use screws
of galvanized iron or brass to hold the
various sections of the box together.

It cannot be emphasized too often
that drainage holes are essential. They
should be about 1·3cm (½in) in diameter.
Drill a double row of holes with roughly
15cm (6in) between the holes in each
row. A window box on a high sill that
is not securely fixed can be most
dangerous, so use long hasps and staple
fittings to secure the box to the window
frame. Where the window ledge has a

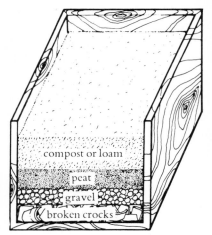

downward and outward slope, use a batten of wood to level the box.

Another way of securing a window box, especially high above the ground, is by a hook and eye arrangement. The eye can be secured to the side of the box and the hook to the window frame. This makes it easy to remove the box. Alternatively the box may be cemented to the wall. Many boxes are now seen hung below the windows, because this is the only way of attaching them to flats, office buildings and houses which have outward opening casement windows and no sills.

Attaching these is hardly within the scope of the usual do-it-yourself enthusiast, even if you are only on the second rather than the nineteenth floor. The advantage is that the plants do not shut out the light, however exuberant they become, and are very easy to look after, but you have to be extra careful about drips because the bottom of the boxes will be out of reach.

Preparation and planting
Prepare the boxes for planting when they are positioned on the sill. (These instructions are equally appropriate for large tubs and urns.) This saves carrying a heavy box full of soil to a window ledge, often in an awkward position, which will need some manoeuvering to get properly sited. (Where galvanized inner linings are to be used in fixed boxes, this is not necessary.)

Lay broken crocks on the bottom of the box about 1·3cm (½in) deep to prevent soil being washed out of the drainage holes and at the same time provide extra drainage. If you have difficulty in getting broken crocks, use pieces of polystyrene, pebbles or small flint stones. On top of this a fibrous material such as peat, which helps to retain moisture, should be laid at a depth of 5cm (2in).

Fill in the rest of the box to within 1·3cm (½in) of the rim with a good texture soil, rich in humus and plant nutrients. This can be potting compost, or you can mix up three parts loam (or good garden soil), one part of peat or leafmould and one part of sharp sand. To each bushel add two or three handfuls of bonemeal. A loamless or 'soilless' compost can also be used. These soils will not need crocks or drainage material in the base of the box—just drainage holes. Give a good soaking before planting and be sure to read the instructions on the bag before you do anything. (If you want to specialize with particular types of plants, you must make their beds to suit their individual needs—acid, sandy, or whatever they may be.)

The soil should be changed every two or three years, or the top 5 to 8cm (2 to 3in) should be replaced with fresh compost or soil. Where there is heavy air pollution, you may need to change the soil every year—the behaviour of the

Left: When planting a window box firm tall plants in before putting in smaller edging plants. Below: Water pot or container plants with a small can to avoid dislodging the soil.

plants will let you know if this is urgent. However, as a precaution, if you feel your plants are at risk, a few nuggets of charcoal in the compost will absorb noxious gases and keep the soil sweet and healthy for a long time.

Fill the window boxes at least a week before you put in the plants so the soil can settle. They like to anchor their roots in a firm new home, rather than grope around in the equivalent of a feather bed to find a foothold.

What to plant

What you plant in any kind of container, and how you arrange them is entirely an individual matter of taste, tempered with what is possible considering eventual height and spread.

Pelargoniums or fuchsias, with alyssum or lobelia, together with foliage plants, such as coleus, or the grey-leaved *Senecio cineraria* will give a summer display needing little attention.

Hardy and half-hardy plants, including stocks, zinnias and verbenas, all give

A more flexible alternative to a window box would be a simple wooden shelf supported on wall brackets on which individual pots can be placed, although it needs to be in a sheltered position. Here tobacco plants (nicotiana) join the ubiquitous pelargoniums, adding their warm scent to this sun room in the evening.

a long-lasting display, if the dead heads, plus stalks, are cut off regularly. Tobacco plants, French and African marigolds, also make a good, if obvious, splash.

Less orthodox planting includes begonias (both tuberous and fibrous-rooted species), ferns, fuchsias, creeping Jenny (*Lysimachia nummularia*) with periwinkles, *Tradescantia fluminensis*, and the smaller ornamental ivies, all of which are suitable for a north-facing aspect.

Where there is partial shade only (north-east and north-west aspects or under dappled shade from trees) begonias, pelargoniums, lobelia, alyssum and

phacelias all do well. For full sunlight, you can use combinations of French and African marigolds; *Salvia splendens*; such pelargoniums as 'Paul Crampel', 'Gustav Emich' and 'Henry Jacoby', contrasted with the silvery foliage of *Helichrysum frigidum* and *H. angustifolium*, or the scarlet petunia 'Comanche' with paler zinnias.

By using shrubs, conifers and pot plants, it is possible to obtain a more rapid display. Cyclamens, cinerarias, schizanthus and primulas are excellent, but the first three need a sheltered south-facing position. Pot chrysanthemums

are tougher, provided they have been hardened off and been out of doors from spring to late autumn, and often into winter.

Whether you are growing plants in window boxes, tubs, barrels or pots, a contrast in their behaviour usually gives the best effect, and creepers and climbers take up little root space for what they give in the way of frills and skirts. Creeping Jenny, canary creeper, nasturtiums and ivy-leaved geraniums are all easy and decorative in a sunny spot, and trailing *Campanula fragilis* can be induced to give a fine display in late summer.

Containers are so generally used as a convenient way of keeping a continuous display of bedding plants in their place —or rather a place convenient to you— that it is mostly forgotten that they can house anything that goes up, down or sideways which does not demand a great root-run.

*Top left: Black-eyed Susan (*Thunbergia alata*) is a pretty climbing plant for container growing.*
Below left: Plant tubs such as this were once used for growing orange trees. They are fitted with lifting rings at the corners to enable them to be moved under cover before the first frosts.

Above: A whitewashed tub contains vivid pink hydrangeas. Above right: Half a barrel has been stripped and varnished and the metal rings smartly polished. Its effective planting includes eucalyptus, petunias and a small birch tree.

Window boxes, or containers on balconies or at the foot of walls, make ideal bases for climbing plants to escape from and make their way up walls, or around windows, given the right support. Some climbers cling naturally to anything they can get a grip on; others need wires or a frame to which they have to be tied as they travel.

Cobea scandens is an outstanding half-hardy climber which will scale 10m (30ft) in one season. The golden-leaved hop, *Humulus japonicus aureus*, is another quick and easy, though less exuberant, climber.

Climbing nasturtiums are very good value, try the scarlet 'Lucifer' and the rich red 'Indian Chief'. Of all the half-hardy climbers, *Ipomoea rubro-caerula* 'Heavenly Blue' (morning glory) must be the most spectacular, if you can give it a sheltered, sunny position. The convolvulus-like flowers open their immense blue trumpets in the morning and fade with the sun.

More permanent climbers are the compact ivies, such as *Hedera helix* *aureo-variegata* or the smaller-leaved 'Buttercup'. There are many beautiful vines, and also the Virginia creeper, *Parthenocissus quinquefolia*, and smaller leaved varieties.

Bulbs make admirable link-men in any kind of outdoor container. They can be brought on in the house until almost ready to flower, or the hardy ones can be planted direct, to come up in their own time among permanent evergreens, or dispensable biennials. By careful planning you can have a show of bulbs at all times of the year. They are also an economy. They will forgive you for removing them from public sight when they fade if you keep them in a cool pot of soil till they dry off naturally, and leave them in an airy, mouse-free place till they are ready to be planted up again and can gradually take sips of water.

Try winter aconite, autumn crocus, glory of the snow, spring crocus, grape hyacinth, Roman hyacinth, narcissi, and the smaller species—scilla, snowdrop and tulip.

Improvised containers

If you cannot afford to spend much on ornamental vases, urns and boxes, or if you simply enjoy looking around for the more unusual types of containers—you will find there is plenty of choice. Old chimney-pots, plain or decorated, make excellent containers, but they will need concrete bases and drainage holes: put in wooden plugs before the concrete has set and knock them out afterwards. Alternatively wedge a large pot inside the top.

Old domestic water tanks of various shapes and sizes look particularly well painted, and it is easy to knock holes in the bases. Look for old wash coppers (if the price has not soared into the antique sphere). Many have rounded bases, and although these can be flattened by gentle hammering they lose much of their character. They are best supported by an iron tummy-band and tripod legs, or by plinths of brick or rock. It is unnecessary to paint them as their greenish bronze appearance is most attractive.

Farm sales are a treasure trove of containers—you will find cast iron feeding troughs in all sizes and hay racks either straight, or for corners, can be lined.

Elderly wooden wheelbarrows, now replaced by lighter ones of metal or plastic, need a few holes drilling in the bottom. They can be left in a natural state, stained or painted. If they are not too near collapse, they have the great advantage of being movable. Old baths, including hip baths, are often amusing features of town gardens, and hollowed-out tree stumps, and painted tractor tyres are more country favourites: even an old-fashioned galvanized coal scuttle, painted white, and overflowing with petunias, can be charming.

Whatever container you choose for your miniature garden, make sure the base is clear of the ground, either with bricks or blocks of wood, to make sure the drainage holes do not get blocked, and to prevent worms and slugs from climbing into the roots.

Below: An example of the large number of different containers available, from simple flower pots to zinc troughs and cider barrels.

HANGING
BASKETS

*Hanging baskets are the perfect situation
for trailing plants. Above: A delightful
mixed cottage garden arrangement.
Opposite: Asparagus Sprengeri cascades
down from this more formal style of
hanging basket.*

Hanging baskets are movable miniature gardens, floating in the air, at or above eye level, showing off, and spilling their contents of bloom and foliage in all directions. They are usually treated as summer decoration, overflowing with brilliant annual flowers; to be tipped out in autumn and planted anew the following spring. They can however be used throughout the year with careful plantings of semi-permanent inhabitants and interlacings of evergreens and house-plants.

The baskets are a delightful way to grow plants where there is no space for them on the ground, particularly in a paved area too small for tubs or boxes. The essence of baskets is that they should have both trailing and upright plants in them so that seen from below, or from a slight distance, there is a definite shape, and not just an untidy jumble of plants.

Positioning the basket

A hanging basket is the quickest way to transform a porch, verandah or entrance hall from a dull to a gay spot. It has the same effect as a flower arrangement, with the great advantage that it will last as long as it is planned to, and never has the studied, static appearance of 'arrangements'. The plants flow, and alter as they grow, and successive flowerings bring constant colour changes.

Given enough light and filled with an appropriate selection of plants, flowering baskets can be hung—almost with abandon—in limitless ways and places. Hang them on strong brackets or chains from a house wall, porch, pergola, balcony, along a fence or other woodwork, from the branches or trees, on the brackets of outdoor lamps or from the rafters of garden rooms. Indoors they brighten up any hallway, sun room or house extension.

Be careful never to put baskets in a draught. They need air, but not a wind tunnel. Outdoor ones get battered and dry out in a matter of hours in strong winds. Draughts are a particular hazard for baskets in hallways when doors are left open and a breeze suddenly gets up. Keep indoor flowering baskets away from the fumes of heaters or furnaces, and do not put them in dark corners— the plants will sulk and go 'leggy' unless given plenty of light.

Choosing a container

There are baskets of many sizes, usually measuring 30 to 45cm (12 to 18in) made of galvanized or plastic-covered wire, as well as semi-circular ones which can be fixed flush to a wall. There are also wicker baskets of many shapes and sizes for indoors, and wooden baskets for outdoors, but these are heavier than other types, and can therefore be impracticable for many people and places. Small pottery hanging containers can sometimes be obtained as well and these are particularly suitable for use indoors.

Weight and size are the most important considerations when choosing your hanging container. It will be much larger when filled with plants branching out in all directions, and may need more space than you had planned for. It will also be *much* heavier. Small containers are easy to cope with but dry out very quickly and need constant watering. However, when choosing larger ones, remember that you must be able to swing them aloft, as well as get them down again for 'maintenance work'. A

Hanging baskets can contain a single species or mixed groups.
Opposite: Fuchsia looks charming seen from below.
Below left: A vivid ivy-leaved pelargonium adds interest to a dull brick wall.
Below right: Mixed baskets are suspended from a garden shed, partially obscuring it from view.

35

Planting a hanging basket.
Right: The basket is balanced on
the rim of a bucket to keep it
firm while planting is carried out.
Far right: An interlining of
plastic is put in place, and holes
punched half way. up to draw off
the surplus water each time
watering is done.
Opposite page, top left: Compost
is put into the basket so that the
finished level will be just above
the polythene lining.
Opposite, below left: Small plants
are knocked out of pots and
planted at an angle in the centre
of the basket.
Opposite, top right: Smaller
plants are put around the sides
and positioned horizontally.
Opposite, below right: The plants
are watered in once the basket is
complete, then left to rest over
the bucket for a few days before
hanging in position.

45cm (18in) basket is the most comfortable size, both for the plants and their maintenance. A pulley is the simplest way of keeping baskets within easy reach for watering, feeding and dead-heading, particularly for the elderly.

The baskets can be lined in the traditional way with sphagnum moss, putting the cleanest parts on the outside, and filling in with potting compost to which two or three handfuls of peat are added for each basket. This keeps weeds at bay, which are difficult to prize out without disturbing the close-growing plants. Or you can use a soilless compost, thoroughly moistened so that it holds together when you squeeze it. This filling will need an occasional feeding boost after the first six weeks, but it is generally lighter in weight than ordinary potting compost.

As an alternative to moss, baskets may be lined with black or green plastic sheeting with a few holes punched in the bottom for drainage. The compost filling will not need watering as often as when lined with moss, but the plastic does give an unnatural appearance, since, however cunningly you put in the plants, some of the plastic is bound to show.

Dripping can be a problem, particularly in a carpeted area, from a town balcony above a pavement or in a doorway. In these circumstances drip trays are essential, even if the baskets are lined with plastic instead of moss, as this has to be perforated at the bottom to allow for drainage, and prevent the contents from becoming a squalid bog. Thin plastic baskets can be bought with a drip tray attached to the base.

Planting a basket
To fill a basket easily, rest it in the top of a bucket or pot so that it is secure. Baskets can be planted either right across the wide top, when filled, or in stages round the sides and through the mesh as you fill them with compost. This will depend on the effect you want and the types of plant you use.

For a gradual build-up, put 8 to 10cms (3 to 4in) of your chosen compost into the lined basket, part the moss and thread the plants sideways between the wires, pressing compost over the roots. Continue at intervals all round until nearing the top. This gives baskets, particularly small ones, a more 'dressed' look, as the basket itself is well hidden from the start and does not have to wait for top-planted trailing plants to act as cover-ups. Do not fill the baskets right to the top of the lining: leave about 2·5cm (1in) and make a shallow depres-

sion at the centre so that water will soak in and not spill over.

Put upright growing plants towards the centre, with the trailers round the outside and small plants in between. But never overplant the baskets or the plants will have to fight each other for survival as they grow bigger, which would make a very sorry sight. Give them a really good soaking when planting is completed, and leave them to rest in a cool airy spot for about a week,

to recover and settle into their new surroundings. They can then take their place in the sun. It is an easy matter to plant a basket, but so often the result falls sadly short of the conception. You need discipline before you choose what to put in them.

In fact, some of the most effective summer baskets contain just one type of flower in a single colour—flame-coloured geraniums, blue petunias, white campanulas, yellow nasturtiums.

Alternatively a fine show of mixed plants and colours can look very effective if the colour balance is carefully arranged.

There is really no limit to what you can grow in a hanging basket. It is not even confined to flowers—anything from alpine strawberries to purple podded climbing beans will survive, so long as their roots have enough nourishment.

It is a matter of choosing what you want for the right place and purpose. Any summer bedding plants and annuals are as happy in the air as on the ground, and will flower freely in full sun. Choose such things as verbenas, dwarf phlox, dwarf French marigolds, dwarf sweet peas, zonal geraniums, mesembryanthemums, and a new trailing lobelia 'Red Cascade' and *Convolvulus minor*.

For more shaded positions, sheltered from wind, but in dappled, not complete shade, there is a wonderful range of trailing begonias in rich glowing colours. Fuchsias like semi-shade too, and the pendulous varieties are at their best when they can be seen from below, weeping their beauty over the edge of the basket.

For the top of a mixed basket, there is a choice of white marguerites, zonal geraniums, yellow calceolarias. One of the best basket trailers is *Asparagus Sprengeri*, with hanging fronds.

Perennials can be planted in baskets, to give leafy decoration in winter—try creeping Jenny (*Lysimachia nummularia*), ivies, ferns and periwinkle (vinca). These can be livened up during summer with any exuberant annuals. These can be removed in autumn and replaced with small flowering spring bulbs and dwarf tulips.

General maintenance

With all this intensive growing and flowering in a confined space, feeding is as necessary as constant watering. Give them a liquid feed every one to three weeks according to growth and development. The feeds come in as many forms as medical cures and tonics —tablets, granules, concentrated liquids.

Take your pick from any garden shop, and read the instructions carefully.

Watering should be thorough. Put your finger in the compost and if it is dry give a thorough soaking. It is best to take the basket down and stand it in a bucket of rainwater, if this is feasible. The soil or compost will need renewing about once a year with perennial plantings.

To keep baskets in shape at all times, remove dead heads and dead leaves, trim back or pinch out the growing tips of anything getting out of hand. Don't be afraid of adding new bedding plants during the summer if the originals look sickly, or you change your mind about liking them. You are master of the basket.

Opposite: An old-fashioned conservatory is a traditional place for hanging baskets particularly of shade-loving plants. Below: Browallia, a greenhouse flowering annual, makes a decorative trailing plant for a hanging basket. Left: Alpine strawberries can be grown in hanging baskets.

GROWING BONSAI

*Bonsai is true miniaturization of nature.
Real trees, not dwarf species, are kept
small by rigorous pruning of branches
and roots. Above: Chamaecyparis
psifera. Left: A collection including
deciduous and flowering species.*

Above: Although bonsai trees such as this have the appearance of great age, it is possible, by careful training, to produce specimens in a few years. Conifers are traditionally used for this technique. Right above: Pinus Sylvestris has been grown at an angle and placed in a tiny container to make an interesting overall shape. Right: Several small specimens of Chamaecyparis psifera are grown together with rocks and moss for a mountainous landscape.

THE WORD BONSAI comes from the Japanese 'bon' meaning pan, and 'sai', a plant. It is the art of dwarfing and shaping trees, growing them in shallow trays so that they remain miniature replicas of their natural counterparts in the wild. Some specimens live to be hundreds of years old, and certainly reach the same age as their free-growing relatives. But often the bonsai will live longer because it does not have to brave the hazards of nature or the extremes of weather. The constant pampering and attention necessary to keep a bonsai alive and dwarfed also adds to its lifespan.

It all started in Japan centuries ago. The first bonsai were dug from high mountains and cliffs where they had become dwarfed, twisted and tortured in to extraordinary shapes by the elements and root restrictions. People who came across them dug them up, and planted them in pots at home, to be admired without the risks of cliff-hanging and mountain climbing. The Japanese were so fascinated by these rare, ancient, gnarled, small-scale specimens that demand soon outstripped supply. This led to shortcutting the natural dwarfing process by a hundred or more years. Japanese gardeners started shaping and training seedlings to imitate what natural deprivation and hardship had done to their ancestors. The first bonsai specialists concentrated on producing grotesque and crippled shapes. This wizened and crippled look has now given way to a more modern taste for charming artistic shapes, rather than anguished ones. No longer is the bonsai in its container a miniature freak of nature, but a natural tree in miniature. These cost comparatively little to buy. The older rare specimens can still occasionally be seen, and can command fabulous prices.

Bonsai enthusiasts usually start with a ready-trained tree in a shallow container obtained from a garden centre or shop, complete with instructions. Specialist nurseries offer a wide choice in their advertisements which are still not expensive compared with the truly venerable.

Growing bonsai

A 'ready-made' bonsai is not as satisfying as creating your own individual, unique tree. Almost any type of tree or shrub can be dwarfed, and strangely, the most successful are those which would normally grow to a large size. They can be grown from seed, a cutting, or a wild seedling if you can find one on a rocky hillside, its roots and growth already stunted.

By far the most exciting of these alternatives is to grow bonsai from seed. It takes longer, but you are in sole control from the start, and can watch over each stage of the development and shape it as the fancy takes you.

Most tree seeds are germinated in spring, either bought from specialist nurseries or the catalogues of general seed houses. The most adventurous as well as the cheapest way is to collect them from beneath mature trees in mid-winter. Many will germinate quickly, in a few weeks, but those with a hard crust will need to be nicked with a knife if there has not been enough frost to soften them while they lay exposed on the ground during winter.

Sow the seed in shallow trays or boxes of soil and leafmould. (Ideally this should be collected from under a tree or from a moist, leaf-lined ditch.) But if this is impracticable, suitable composts can be bought at little cost, since only a small quantity is needed for each individual miniature tree. Put the tray outside in a cold frame or under a cloche or similar protection. A glass or plastic sheet leaning against a sheltered house wall on a balcony will serve equally well, with the sheet raised slightly for good ventilation.

A simple and well-proven way of germinating a bonsai is to use half a grapefruit or orange skin, having scooped out the fruit. Pierce the sides in several places with a skewer, fill almost to the top with soil and leafmould, and press the tree seed into the middle of it. Water the soil and put into a plastic bag, sealed at the top in a tent shape, leaving space for air. Put it into a dark, warm cupboard, where it is not likely to be forgotten, and the moment a shoot emerges through the soil, remove the grapefruit and put it in full light, but not into strong sun. Never let the soil dry out, and as the roots start to grow through the holes in the skin, snip them off with scissors. Root restriction is part of the dwarfing process, as it limits the amount of nourishment the plant can take. The little seedling still in its fruit case can be put into its permanent container with more leafmould and soil added after the first crop of roots have been sheared, and training of top growth will have to start. The advantage of the grapefruit shell is that it makes it easy to lift from its permanent container and nip off any roots which penetrate through.

Seeds germinating in trays should be

Ways of obtaining different shapes for bonsai.
1. Upright with a simple cane or dowelling stake.
2. Oblique, by twisting heavy gauge wire round the trunk. (The container should be fairly heavy to counter-balance the tree.)
3. Cascading style. Stout string should be tied round the trunk and under the container to start with, to keep the roots in the compost.
4 and 5. Wiring branches to change the direction of their growth.

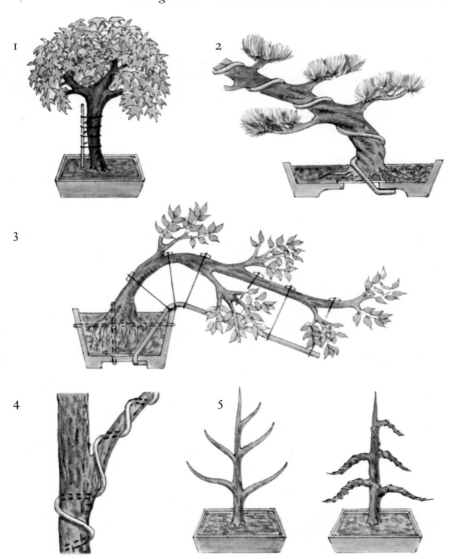

left to grow at least 2·5cm (1in) tall before they are pricked out into individual little posts—peat, plastic, waxed paper, half orange or grapefruit skins—and put back into the frame or a sheltered spot, surrounded by moist peat.

Training bonsai

Proper training begins when the seedling is about 7cm (3in) tall. Nip out the growing tip to encourage side shoots and when these in turn become little branches, remove their growing tips when they reach the length you want. Once the tree has a few branches you have to decide whether to continue shaping it to an ancient appearance entirely by pruning, or with wires, or by a combination of both methods.

The safest time to wire is during the growing period. Anchor the wire into the soil and wind it around the main trunk and branches to give whatever windswept or asymmetrical shape pleases you. Leave the wire on until the growth has 'set', but not long enough for it to cut into the bark. You can also weigh down the branches with a tied-on stone right over the edge of the container, or with a hairpin into the soil. However, never do too much to the tree at one time. Growing bonsai is a slow process.

To shape a bonsai entirely by pruning, you pinch or cut branches and shoots to just above a bud on the bark which is already pointing in the way you want it to grow—downwards, sideways, or whatever. A little wiring and pruning will keep you on the safe side. Whatever the method you use, the result will be more pleasing if you do not let more than one branch grow from the main trunk at the same height, so stagger them.

When a seedling plant is a few months old, take it gently from its pot and completely cut off any strong roots. It is the small hairy roots which feed the tree, and these will need only a light trim with scissors. The strong roots are the anchors when the tree is growing in the wild, and if left would ruin the whole bonsai technique. Put the seed-

ling back in the pot immediately and refirm the soil.

For the first year or two you will need to repot, prune the roots and branches, or train with wires, in both spring and autumn. Prune the roots by a third to two-thirds and put the tree back in the same pot or one only slightly larger, and add fresh quick-draining compost, with a little sharp sand added.

**Transferring bonsai
to permanent containers**

After three years, a bonsai tree grown from seed should have settled into an attractive shape and adapted to the niggling treatment you are giving it. It is ready to graduate from the nursery bed to a permanent container. This

Below: Pruning techniques.
1. Root pruning
2. Top pruning

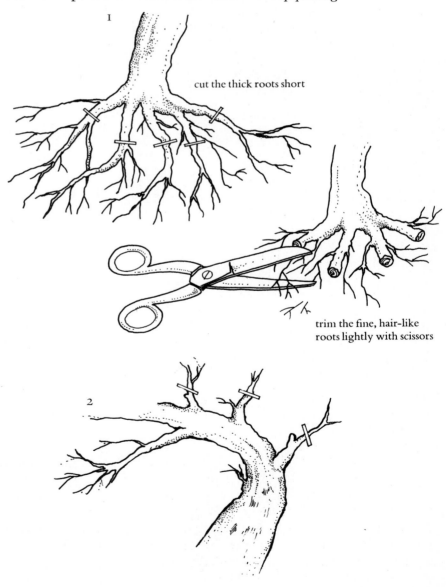

cut the thick roots short

trim the fine, hair-like roots lightly with scissors

Bonsai are essentially decorative plants—in Japan their cultivation is considered an art. Their containers should be utterly simple—the natural texture of stone or earthenware in basic circular or rectangular shapes, but with hard edges softened by curves. Although a group such as this could be displayed indoors very effectively, it is wise to give them the benefit of fresh air from time to time. Most bonsai trees are grown from hardy evergreen species which under normal circumstances would be used to the rigours of an exposed mountainside. Don't stifle them permanently in a dry, centrally heated atmosphere.

must be chosen most carefully although of course it is very much a matter of personal taste. Remember, however, that it could outlive you! It should be shallow and have drainage holes, and preferably be of a natural colour to blend with your particular choice of specimen. Shades of stone brown, white, charcoal and green give good results. A round or oval container is most suited to a single, up-standing bonsai, but when several are to be grown together, or when a cascade effect is the aim, a rectangular shape generally sets off the plants to best advantage. In most cases bonsai thrive better in completely unglazed containers, but small ones, glazed only on the outside, are quite trustworthy when you get to know the plants' water requirements.

Spread out the roots of the bonsai in the chosen container and sift the soil over them shaking the plant gently from the base of the trunk. Press lightly at the same time to make sure there are

A selection of singly planted bonsai showing the great variety of sizes possible. If you grow your own bonsai you can determine its size according to the situation in which it is to be placed.

48

no air pockets, and that all the fine hair roots are covered and in contact with the compost. If the bonsai seems unsteady or top-heavy at first in its shallow living room, weigh down one or two roots with rocks or attractive flints or stones. These can be left permanently, if they add to the overall appearance, once the plant has settled in.

Care of the established bonsai

From now on the pruning and shaping should be necessary only in spring. Many people think that root pruning keeps a bonsai dwarfed. In fact, it helps very little towards this aim, and is done to strengthen the little tree by encouraging the growth of the fine feeding roots. When root-pruning an established bonsai, take it carefully from the container, brush away some of the soil, and, with scissors, cut out completely any new thick roots which have developed, and merely snip the tips of the hair roots, just as in their nursery stage.

Never do too much at one time to a bonsai. If a whole branch needs removing, do not do anything else for some months, either above or below the soil. Less major operations such as leaf and shoot pruning and pinning down should be done 'little and often'. Bonsai are not demanding plants. They need only enough attention to keep you interested in them all through the year.

As a general guide, repot fruit and flowering species every year in spring, deciduous trees every two to three years, and evergreens every four to five years.

Starvation is not to be recommended as a cut-price way of keeping a bonsai dwarfed; it will die. They need regular meals, not so rich that they produce too much sappy growth, but just enough to keep them going. Bonsai differ in their needs, but a general guide would be a dose of liquid fertilizer once a week from spring to autumn, and a slower acting granular or powder fertilizer once a month. Nothing should be given

Cotoneaster horizontalis has tiny pink flowers in summer, and bright red berries in autumn. Its small box-like leaves and natural trailing habit make it particularly suitable for bonsai culture.

during the winter months.

Watering plays one of the most important parts in bonsai cultivation, although it is impossible to lay down hard and fast rules for different types. The roots must never be allowed to dry out, but over-watering can be even more disastrous. If they become water-logged the soil becomes airless and sour, and the roots literally drown. A general guide would be once a week in winter, once a day in spring, two or three times a day during summer and once or twice a week in autumn. But much will depend on where the plants are positioned. If possible use rain water. When tap water is the only choice, leave it in the open air for 24 hours before using. Trees in extremely shallow containers or growing singly will need the most attention, particularly in hot weather. Use a fine spray to avoid dislodging the soil and keep watering until the water seeps through the drainage hole. Deciduous trees need more summer watering than evergreens and should never be sprayed when they are in hot sun, or the leaves will be scorched.

Keeping bonsai indoors

Although the natural home of bonsai trees is in the open air, they can be brought into the house for a few days at a time if you keep to a few 'do's and don'ts'. Keep them in plenty of light but not in a high temperature. Do not stand them in a saucer of water or the roots will rot. Spray two or three times a day in hot, dry weather. They cannot be kept in a centrally heated room more than a few days as they *must* have fresh air. In summer the plants can put up with indoor life longer, a week or so, because doors and windows are open. In winter the atmosphere in the house is usually too dry and hot, so take care when and where you bring it indoors.

In cold weather, before returning a tree outside after a spell indoors, cool it off each night in a cold room. When outdoors, they should be protected from all extremes: burning sun, fog, severe frost or cold winds. In winter the pot can be buried beneath the soil and generally needs no further attention. However, in extreme weather it is advisable to cover the surface of the soil around the trunk with straw or dead bracken. Most specimens are completely hardy but will not enjoy being entirely exposed for the whole of winter.

A covered patio or porch, or even a car port, gives enough light and protection from what the winter might bring, without any 'molly-coddling' which invariably does more harm than good. In heavy frost, loose straw, sacking, or netting can be put round the container, and in extremely bad weather, over the whole plant. Alternatively, you could bring it inside until the worst is over.

Species to grow

The choice of the trees and shrubs you can grow in bonsai form is vast. As well as juniper, acers, silver birch, cedars, pine, oak, sycamore, ash, hornbeam, horse chestnut, hazel and walnut, there are many which bloom charmingly, and while resting in winter, naked, are equally attractive in silhouette and shade and shape of bark. These include cherries, crab apple, laburnum and wisteria. Others, like the cotoneasters, produce bright scarlet berries and autumn tinted foliage. One of the most fascinating of the deciduous trees is the Maidenhair Tree, Ginkgo, a rare survivor from prehistoric times. It grows rapidly from seed, reaching up to 1m (3ft) in 18 months, which puts it out of bounds for some purposes, but its ornate lime-green leaves and shape of growth appeal to anyone who sees it. In its natural environment it reaches 30m (60ft).

All these can be grown from seeds which are rarely expensive. You can also buy mixed packets of conifer and deciduous tree seeds. The latter include conical and wide spreading forms, small leaved types and flowering varieties. The conifers are a skilfully chosen mixture of pine, cedar, juniper, spruce, fir, and many more with other types of growth, such as weeping, pyramidal, horizontal and spreading. For an outlay of only a few pennies, you can afford to make a few mistakes while you learn the art, and cannot fail to have some successes.

Whatever type or size of bonsai you create, and irrespective of whether they are in individual trays, or grouped in a single container to give a miniature garden effect, they should be placed at a level to be seen at their best, something of lasting value of which you can be deservedly proud.

Acers (maple) are among the many deciduous trees suitable for bonsai treatment. This is Acer pseudo-platanus, the leaves of which have a pinkish tinge when they first appear in spring.

BOTTLE GARDENS, TERRARIA, WARDIAN CASES

The self-contained environment of the bottle garden or Wardian case is the perfect setting for tender, moisture-loving plants. The use of foliage plants such as coleus (above) adds colour.

BOTTLE GARDENS, terraria and Ward, or Wardian, cases are all basically the same thing. They are virtually self-contained worlds needing little attention once they are planted, and, in the case of air-tight versions, they are entirely self-perpetuating.

Most leafy plants from warm countries need, in cultivation, not only heat but humidity. This vital component of growth—not to be confused with soil moisture—is the most difficult to understand, because it is invisible and not readily discernible, while the instrument which measures its concentration—the hygrometer—is not a standard piece of equipment.

In a greenhouse, air moisture is provided by 'damping down' the floor, staging, or both. But when we come to cultivate these plants in rooms, air dryness becomes a serious problem, because all our methods of room heating tend to dry out the air excessively. To enclose room plants within glass was a logical step.

The principle of enclosed cultivation has an interesting history which also explains the slight difference between the types. Nathaniel Ward, a London doctor and naturalist living in the first half of the nineteenth century, discovered the plant-growing case named after him. Wishing to study a chrysalis he brought back from the countryside, he buried it in some soil in an almost airtight glass jar. He noticed that seeds in the soil soon began to germinate, forming plants which grew vigorously. He continued making experiments and in 1838 he made the first Wardian case from metal and glass. The principle was soon used to make fern-cases in which these moisture-loving plants could be grown indoors inside the case even if the surrounding atmosphere was dry. It also enabled living plants to be dispatched successfully over long distances when transport was slow and difficult. It was used by Robert Fortune when he made his plant-collecting expedition to China in 1845. Later, it made possible the introduction of tea plants to India, the world-wide distribution of quinine-

producing plants and the first cultivation of bananas outside China.

Wardian cases became a feature of many Victorian homes and sometimes became quite intricate in their design—like miniature versions of Crystal Palace or the Palm House at Kew Gardens. However, apart from their practical use as plant transporters, they became fashionable early this century and few original ones now exist. On page 60 there is an example of a modern Wardian Case to suit a twentieth century home.

During the 1940s the same principle was applied in the USA to an indoor gardener's 'gimmick'—growing plants in a bottle. This has now become so popular that planted bottles are sold commercially.

The standard bottle for gardening is the large, round carboy which until recently was used for acid and distilled water (now they are being replaced by plastic containers). Oval carboys and the vertical-sided demijohn used for spirits are also attractive. In fact any bottle can be used as long as its aperture is large enough to allow plants to be inserted.

Terraria are basically the same as bottle gardens—they can be any glass container other than a bottle in which it is possible to grow plants. A perfect example is a fish tank, particularly one with built-in fluorescent lights which can enhance the display in a room setting. In the nineteenth century, keen amateurs actually constructed aquaterraria—part miniature greenhouse for plant growing and part aquarium for fish!

Terraria have a distinct advantage over bottle gardens in that a great variety of flowering plants can be grown in them—their simple shape makes it easy to remove dead flowerheads which should not be allowed to rot inside the container.

Cultivating a bottle garden

Bottling plants is much easier than the final result may lead one to imagine—certainly simpler than putting a ship in a bottle! After cleaning the carboy

The Wardian case was a feature of many Victorian homes, and was often used to house ferns in a completely enclosed world. They were often very ornate, such as the fine example illustrated here, and are now considered to be collectors' items.

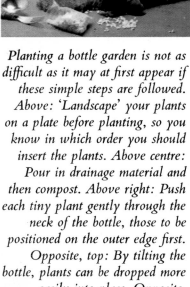

Planting a bottle garden is not as difficult as it may at first appear if these simple steps are followed. Above: 'Landscape' your plants on a plate before planting, so you know in which order you should insert the plants. Above centre: Pour in drainage material and then compost. Above right: Push each tiny plant gently through the neck of the bottle, those to be positioned on the outer edge first. Opposite, top: By tilting the bottle, plants can be dropped more easily into place. Opposite, below: Use improvised tools—an old spoon and fork bound to the ends of canes—to manipulate plants, and arrange compost in the bottle. Opposite, far right: Final decorations such as pebbles can be added using a long cardboard tube as a funnel.

thoroughly a 2·5cm (1in) deep layer of small crocks is inserted. This is followed by soil, which can be poured in through a paper funnel or a cardboard tube to avoid soiling the glass. A good mixture consists of 1 part fibrous loam, 2 parts of peat and 1 part of coarse sand, or 2 parts of an ordinary potting compost and 1 part of extra peat can be mixed. The soil mixture should be just damp, by no means wet, and the soil layer should be 12 to 15cm (5 to 6in) deep.

The only tools needed are a cane with a cotton reel pushed firmly on to one end and a length of 2·5cm (1in) wide wooden lath, pointed at one end. Small plastic tools, a trowel at one end, a fork or rake at the other, are sold for use by indoor gardeners. If these are cut in half and the cut-ends pushed into lengths of cane, two useful tools can be made for use when the bottle is being prepared and planted. With the cotton reel the soil is firmed down; the flat end of the lath is used to push the soil about and the pointed end to excavate planting holes. It is essential to make each hole large enough to accommodate the roots of the plant destined for it. It may be necessary to take some soil off the root ball before it can be passed through the neck of the bottle.

Start with the plants around the outside of the bottle (to avoid dropping soil on those already planted). Push the root ball through the aperture, then hold the plant by its leaves, push it gently through and let it drop. It can then be pushed into its hole with the cane and lath (or with the plastic tools),

the roots covered with soil, and the cotton reel used to make the plants firm.

Plants should be purchased in the smallest pots available. One large firm specializing in house plants, supplies small specimens intended for use in bottle gardens. Suitable plants are: *Calathea oppenheimiana, C. ornata, C. zebrina; Cryptanthus bivittatus, C. tricolor* and others; *Fittonia argyroneura, F. verschaffeltii; Maranta leuconeura Kerchoveana, M. Massangeana, M. makoyana; Neanthe bella; Peperomia magnoliaefolia, P. caperata, P. hederaefolia, P. sandersii* and others; *Vriesia splendens.* Ferns such as *Asplenium nidus* and *Pellaea rotundifolia* are suitable. Rampant growers such as tradescantia must be avoided, and flowering plants are more trouble than they are worth.

Little attention is needed once the bottle garden is planted. If the neck is sealed, little or no water is needed (plants have been known to flourish in bottle gardens for several years with no extra water added from the time of planting), but condensation will form on the glass at certain times; this gradually clears as the moisture runs down the inside of the glass into the soil. This is, in fact, a continual cycle; water given off through the leaves of the plants in the form of vapour, condenses on the glass, runs back into the soil, is absorbed again through the roots of the plants and is again given off through the foliage. If the bottle is open a cupful of water every month or so in summer is desirable. Dead leaves are removed by cutting them off with a piece of razor-

blade wired to a cane; they can then be lifted out on a pointed cane. This is important to avoid rotting and fungal growth which could spread quickly in the warm, humid atmosphere. Keep the bottle out of direct sunlight, but make sure that it is in good indirect light.

Exactly the same principles, but less trouble, can be used if you want to plant a large goldfish bowl, a brandy glass, a wide-necked jar, or a pan which is then covered by a bell glass.

Cultivating terraria or Wardian cases

The openings of terraria are generally nearly the same size as the growing area so planting is a great deal easier than for bottle gardens, although the same general rules apply. There is no need to use tiny plants and the range is less limited. Many people like to arrange terraria or Wardian cases as miniature landscapes with pieces of interesting driftwood or small rocks interspersed with plants and flowers. Plants can even be left in their pots, standing on a layer of pebbles and the surface covered in with sphagnum moss. Small orchids can be grown this way very effectively. Dwarf varieties such as *Dendrobium aggregatum* or many of the miniature oncidiums are suitable. Miniature pelargoniums are now available and popular in the US, although difficult to find in Britain. Small cuttings constantly

Many different types and sizes of glass container can be used to make bottle gardens. Round carboys or demijohns with fairly wide necks are usually best. Here an old half-gallon cider bottle has been laid on its side for a change of emphasis and an old branch has been inserted with ivies and other creeping plants for a woodland effect. Other useful plants are begonia, pilea, grape ivy or, for tall bottles, sanseveria. African violets (Saintpaulia) can also be grown, although flowering plants are not usually a good idea unless it is easy to remove dead flower heads quickly. If not, the decaying matter will become mouldy and infect the rest of the garden.

thinned could be effective however. They thrive better without too much warmth. Miniature roses and saint-paulias (African violets) are also perfect for terraria—if you have a glass dome or belljar you could grow individual specimens. Ferns are also delightful when grown in this way—their delicately shaped fronds and brilliant green tones can make a very attractive display. They thrive in the humid atmosphere of the terrarium yet generally do not require a great deal of heat.

Finally a word about sealed germination. The original 'cloches' or belljars were in fact aids to the exterior germination and protection of seedlings in early spring when there was still a danger of frost. These were developed into the glass or plastic cloches that are well-known to every keen gardener today. More and more, however, it is being

Right: A modern Wardian case is an attractive way of displaying some of the larger houseplants. Below: This type of bottle garden requires little maintenance—just a little water about every six weeks.

realized that the germination of seeds and the raising of individual seedlings is made quicker and more secure by the use of sealed propagators. These can be large enough for several seed trays or small enough for a single pot. For the small scale gardener who has no greenhouse these are a boon, and will help to raise not only healthy house plants from seeds or cuttings, but also start vegetables or fruit—perhaps for ultimate transplanting into containers.

Terraria and Wardian cases are more flexible than bottle gardens since it is easier to gain access to the plants inside. This unusual terrarium is suspended from a hook on the wall for eye-level viewing.

DISHES, BOWLS AND PLANTERS

*Indoor plants can be grouped together in
dishes or bowls to make delightful, but
semi-permanent, miniature gardens
which also make charming gifts.*

Above: A tiny rock garden of alpines, dwarf conifers and succulents is planted in a small seed tray. Above right: A formal dish garden containing trailing ivy (Hedera) and a stately sanseveria.

DISH AND BOWL gardening is essentially an indoor sport. The usual progression is from growing individual plants in pots in various places around the house, to realizing they show off each other more generously as a group. Any awkward shapes, such as a beautiful flowerhead with a long bare stem, can be disguised or off-set in this case perhaps by the beautiful low-growing foliage of other plants, which either flower insignificantly or not at all.

This is instant gardening at its easiest. The chosen plants can be left in their pots and assembled together, or knocked out and put into peat soil into whatever arrangement you choose. In fact dish gardens can be a more permanent alternative to conventional flower arrangements—they make perfect table centres, for instance.

Earnest gardeners could consider this a slap-happy way of treating plants; here today, out tomorrow. But many plants are expendable, and only intended for a butterfly life of a single season.

Dish and bowl gardens can make excellent and unusual presents, and can be bought ready planted from most florists and garden centres. Unfortunately they are usually in containers which are a great embarrassment once the plants have expired, unless you have the will to re-fill them. Commercial dish gardens often include miniature landscaping and architecture such as pagodas, wishing-wells, rustic bridges and even figures. However, these generally do little to enhance the overall effect of the dish garden.

The home-made product is, by contrast, a joy to assemble and rearrange until you have the creation you want for a particular place in the home.

Containers and their preparation

Containers are of the first importance. Choose them to suit the space and position for which they are intended, before you choose the plants to go into them. Remember that whatever place you want to be decorated with a dish of flowering plants, there must be sufficient light, no direct heat and little draught. Foliage plants, however, allow for more flexibility.

Almost any container can be adapted to suit your personal taste—antique wash-stand sets, gravy boats or large tureens, anything made of china, pottery, terracotta, wood, plastic, fibreglass. In fact almost any material but metal, which can corrode with the action of soil acids.

When using a precious piece of china as a container, whether it is a tiny cream boat or large decorated bowl, do remember that even the stoutest glazes can be stained eventually by the soil. Line a china container with aluminium foil or plastic sheeting, keeping the

The joy of dish gardens is that, given enough resources, you can put in almost any combination of plants. Left: A group of houseplants, all readily available, is dominated by the red bracts of poinsettia. This would make a bright display in winter when cut flowers are generally scarce and expensive. Below left: A group of ferns in a 'rustic' container would be suitable for a cool, moist position, for instance in a bathroom.

edges tucked out of sight, before starting any planting. In this way you can also use cracked or riveted pieces you might otherwise have felt were unusable for the purpose.

Where there are no drainage holes in the container there must be enough depth to allow for a deep layer of drainage material. This can consist of broken flower pots; charcoal crushed into 1·5cm (½in) pieces or even smaller; coarse sand; fine gravel; cinders or clinkers. To stop the soil from sifting immediately into the drainage material, moss or peat will provide a restraining barrier. Take a peep into the soil frequently at different intervals to make sure the drainage material has not become clogged.

The compost or soil is not too important with these indoor arrangements, because in most cases they are transitory.

Planting a miniature rock garden. Top right: The base of the dish is covered with large rocks for drainage, and these are covered with moss and peat. Centre right: Compost is added to about half the depth of the pan, and levelled. Below right: Suitable stones are put in position and firmed in place with a dibber. Far right, top and centre: Small plants are planted with a narrow trowel. Far right, below: The finished garden.

A general mixture of plants will like a mixture of equal parts of sand, loam and well soaked peat.

Planting a dish garden

Have everything ready before you start to plant your container, with the drainage material occupying about a third of the space that the soil will need. Cover this with about 2·5cm (1in) of compost, knock out the first plant from its pot, gently tease away some soil from the roots and ease it gently into the container, spreading out the roots and trickling a little soil over to firm them. Add the other plants at slightly different levels in the soil, so the roots can travel above and below each other without interference. Top finally with soil, making sure there is at least 2·5cm (1in) to spare between the soil surface and the top of the container, for watering.

When arranging pots of plants into containers, the roots will still be restricted and the process different. This method is used mainly when easy replacement is wanted as soon as a flowering plant fades, and the cost is of no importance. The container will have to be deep enough to hide the rims of the pots. Apart from that, all you need is a layer of drainage material, such as gravel, and an interlacing of damp peat to keep the pots steady and moist.

As plants die, or get out of harmony with the other occupants of the dish, you simply remove the offender and add another. The outcast will frequently revive with some personal treatment and be healthy enough to join the dish arrangement at a later date.

Watering and feeding will depend entirely on what you want to grow and the container you choose to put them in. If the plants are temporary and in pots they should need very little extra food. Permanent plants with free roots must have their needs considered individually. Always use a fine spray or indoor can which will soak slowly into the compost, and not dash through it like a waterfall, draining away all the mineral nutrients essential for plant growth.

There is no limit to what you can grow in a bowl in the house. A huge shallow casserole dish can be used temporarily to display groups of spring bulbs, in or out of pots, and nestling in moss or peat. Alternatively the pebble and sand method shown on this page is a novel way to grow bulbs. Or there can be other containers showing off tropical species such as the bromeliads, tender ones, those loving shade but not draught, and hardy plants which will thank you for being out of doors for the warmer part of the year, before being returned to their indoor 'display' routine.

An unusual dish garden of bulbs can be grown on pebbles and water. Top: Shingle or rough sand is bedded at the base of a shallow bowl and the bulbs set upright on it. Above left: Pebbles of roughly the same size are packed around the bulbs to hold them in position while growing. Above: Water is added to about half way up the pebbles. Keep the prepared bowl in a dark place until growth has started, then bring into the light. Top up the water as necessary.

67

Above, left and right: Planters bring growing plants indoors on a larger scale than other methods, and, providing the plants enjoy similar growing conditions, you can plant a wide variety. Right: An unusual method, if you have a suitable overhang or gallery, would be to let trailing plants grow down, forming a natural curtain or room-divider.

Planters

'Planters' are usually larger containers for growing numbers of plants in one place—rather like an indoor window box. They can come in a variety of shapes and sizes, and as with dish and bowl gardens, you can either fill them with compost for direct planting or keep plants in their pots and simply cover the surface with sphagnum moss. Planters are excellent for giving rampant growers their 'heads'—plants like grape ivy (*Rhoicissus rhomboidea*), the delightful sweetheart plant (*Philodendron scandens*); or tradescantia and the tall sansevieria. Alternatively, a group of showy pelargoniums or azaleas in pots in summer could be replaced by forced bulbs to give a touch of spring in winter.

Once again drainage is important—fill a large planter in the same way as a window box or exterior tub, but make sure there is an adequate drip tray.

Any indoor garden where different plants are grouped together is open to cross-infection by pests and diseases. Keep a close watch for symptoms and remove sick plants immediately.

Above: In an open-plan room a planter is kept off the carpeted area. The container is raised on castors for ease of movement. Left: A group of cinerarias in an antique bowl makes a simple but effective dish garden.

CACTI AND SUCCULENTS

*Cacti and succulents are fascinating
plants to grow, and a group of different
species could be combined into a dish or
sink garden with interesting results.
Left: Chiaporia naiada.*

ALL CACTI are succulents, but not all succulents are cacti. The name comes from the latin word *succus*, meaning juice, and is used for plants which have reservoirs in their leaves, stems, flower tubes, and sometimes roots, for storing moisture.

There are succulent plants in a wide variety of plant families, yet one family may have only a few succulents. They are described generally as xerophilous plants, which have evolved structures to cope with long stretches of drought. They are found in nature in areas where there is either little rainfall, or the rain is limited to two or three months of the year. This can vary from sandy desert, dry grassland, to rocky mountain, with tremendous differences of temperature. The hardy succulents of Britain, such as sedums and sempervivums, evolved from mountain areas with little top soil which was often frozen in winter.

The characteristic which distinguishes cacti from other succulents is that they have unique 'cushions' which form in the leaf axils, called aeroles. These are the vital growing areas of cacti and are

clothed variously with spines, bristles, and frequently with a hairy covering.

There are so many different genera and species of succulents that it is not possible to deal with them all here. South Africa is the home of many of the genera grown by collectors, and the USA has many indigenous species.

Because they can withstand considerable drought, succulents are easier to grow than most pot plants. They will not wither or droop when watering is neglected. This is a blessing when you are on holiday as they can be left entirely alone.

Succulents are mostly found in the deserts of the world, and very few are completely hardy in a temperate climate. They have to be given winter protection, or treated permanently as house or greenhouse plants.

Care and cultivation

The few succulents which do not like excessive summer heat in the greenhouse or indoors, can be put outside during the summer months. They must be protected from slugs and insect pests, and watered occasionally during dry weather. If these plants are bedded out for the summer it will be difficult to repot them in the same sized pots when they are taken indoors again. So generally it is better to leave them in their pots when they go out for a summer breather.

However, most succulents can be kept at 4°–7°C (40°–45°F) through the winter, provided the soil is dry, and they can stand any temperature they are likely to encounter during the summer.

During the winter, any cacti or succulents grown as house plants should be kept almost bone dry, being given just sufficient water to keep them plump and healthy. March is the time to start encouraging them into new growth which will induce them to produce their flowers—often surprisingly gay and attractive, yet usually shortlived.

Never begin to feed cacti or succulents until their roots have become accustomed once again to regular moisture. Start to increase their watering gradually, and then begin feeding them in spring. Give them as much light as

Sedum (Stonecrop) and sempervivum (Houseleek) are hardy succulents, commonly grown in rock gardens, but which are equally at home in succulent collections, sink or dish gardens. Left: Sedum roseum. Far left: Sempervivum ciliosum.

possible, always keeping them close to the glass of a south-facing window. If the temperature is too cold outside, bring them back a little into the room, making sure that they will still get the benefit of good light.

The method of watering by immersion is not to be recommended unless the soil is brick hard. If plants are repeatedly dunked in water, most of the nourishment in the soil will be washed out of the drainage hole—when a pot is lifted out of deep immersion, much of the water runs out of the bottom and it contains a lot of soluble food, so there will be little left in the soil of much use to the plant.

A better way of watering a dry and neglected pot is to put it in a container, and pour only a small amount of water into the outer receptacle: just as much as the soil can absorb completely. The amount of water will depend on the size and dryness of the pot. When it is lifted out, no water should run from the bottom.

Most succulents are not at all particular as to the type of soil they are grown in, provided it is porous. Many can be grown in almost pure sand, while others grow better in a fairly rich compost, as long as you remember not to over-water the plant.

It is sometimes recommended that a special soil is used for each genus, but it is possible to grow a varied collection by using one soil only. If you have a large number of plants to pot up, you will no doubt like to mix your own soil. But when you have only a few plants, it is far easier to buy some ordinary potting compost, and add a little extra roughage to make up a suitable mixture. Add a sixth part of coarse sand to five parts of compost. If the sand is not very coarse some extra roughage must be used, such as grit and granulated charcoal. This does not provide food for the plants but makes the compost

Above: Brilliantly coloured when in flower, cacti are not difficult to raise from seed. Right: Echino-cactus, Opuntia and Mamillaria specimens form part of a magnificent collection of cacti and other succulents.

Left: Rhipsalidopsis rosea 'Electra' has pendant pink flowers, produced from the areoles at the ends of the joints. Below: The Easter Cactus, Schlumbergera gaertneri, flowers very freely in spring.

more porous.

Once watering is begun in the early days of spring, enough should be given to ensure that the soil in the pot is well damped. It may be necessary to go over them all again to make sure that the plants have absorbed enough.

Most ordinary pot plants soon indicate when water is needed by their drooping leaves. This warning is not apparent with succulents, even after weeks without watering. To grow the plants successfully you should water fairly regularly, not just when the fancy takes you. But remember that succulents will not survive long in a water-logged soil. So good drainage is essential.

The secret of watering all succulents is to refrain from giving any more water until the soil has dried out. This will depend on the warmth of the living room or greenhouse, and the rate at which the plants grow. More succulents die from over-watering than are ever lost by under-watering.

Repotting

The time for repotting succulents depends on the type. With species which have a resting period, repotting must wait till new growth has begun. Normally early spring would be the time for this task, but some of the genera may be resting then, and so should wait for a few months before being repotted. Most succulents usually benefit from a repotting at least every two years.

Plants in small pots use most of the nourishment in the soil, and so will need a change. Some of those which grow rapidly can be repotted once a year.

When the plant growth reaches the side of the pot, a larger pot is needed. It is important to be able to see or feel the actual soil around the plant, to make certain it needs watering.

When repotting, all the old soil must be discarded. A good crock should almost cover the drainage hole of the pot, and the larger the pot, the easier it will be to remove the plant when repotting again becomes necessary. The compost should be crumbly and moist when repotting is done, and then no water need be given for about a week or more, depending on how long the compost takes to dry out.

Miniature cactus gardens

Cacti make excellent miniature gardens. The container need not have drainage holes, provided it is not overwatered. Place some crocks in the bottom, and only half-fill with a porous soil. When the plants are in position, put in the rest of the soil and press it firm.

An arrangement of cacti and succulents makes a most attractive dish garden which will flourish in a warm room with a dry atmosphere. One of these

Right: Potting a young specimen. Use a spoon to place compost round the plant, then firm with an old knife handle. Below: Cacti can grow to large proportions. In the wild many are as tall as trees. Below right: A really miniature succulent collection is grown in a large shell.

would be particularly suitable in a centrally heated living room. There is a great variety to choose from, and specialist nurseries and garden shops can supply most of the popular species for varied conditions.

To make a dish garden, choose one not less than 2·5cm (2in) deep. Put in drainage material consisting of gravel, small pieces of charcoal, broken crocks, or clinkers. Remove the plants carefully from their pots, arrange them as you wish, put compost between them, firm them in and leave to settle. Carefully

Top: The charming flowers of Opuntia speggazzinii are silvery white and grow in groups. Unfortunately cactus flowers seldom last more than a few days. Left: The individual globular growths of Mammillaria gracilis are offsets from the main plant. These can be removed and planted up singly as a means of propagation.

77

Growing cacti from seed. Top right: The pot is filled with drainage material and then sandy compost. Centre right: Several different types of seeds can be sown in one pot if divided with cardboard in this way. Bottom right: Seedlings will appear at different rates. The ones on the left are ready for pricking out. Far right top: Tiny pots for the individual seedlings need a lot of drainage material. Far right centre: Prick out the tiny seedlings with tweezers made from split bamboo, to avoid damaging them. Far right, bottom: Cacti can also be propagated by grafting offsets onto existing plants

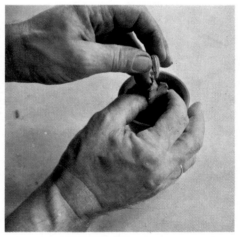

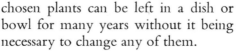

chosen plants can be left in a dish or bowl for many years without it being necessary to change any of them.

Many species of cacti from the following genera grow well on a window ledge: chamaedereus, echinopsis, epiphyllum, gymnocalycium, lobivia, mammillaria and notocactus. A few of the smaller types of cereus can be grown and *C. cleistocactus strausii* will also grow for many years before it gets too large.

These are suitable for bowls with the exception of the epiphyllums, unless they are very small.

Pests and diseases

If cacti are grown well and are healthy, they have little to fear from disease. But there are a few pests which may attack a sick plant. The most frequent is the mealy bug, which appears in a small tuft of wool or powder. Scale may also

attack some cacti and looks like a small scab. Red spider mites can be a nuisance if the atmosphere is too dry. All these pests can be killed with malathion, used strictly as directed.

Propagating succulents

Some succulents can be raised from seed and soon make sizeable plants. Others can be propagated by division or by taking cuttings. Many of the succulent-leaved types can be increased by taking off the leaves and rooting them in sharp sand. When this is done, the leaves should be just laid on the surface of the sand. If the leaves or cuttings are pushed into the sand too deeply they may rot and fail to produce roots.

A small, heated propagating frame is very useful for raising seeds. Half pots of about 10cm (4in) in diameter are very good for sowing small quantities. Using seed compost, put a small quantity through a perforated zinc sieve. Place the coarse material over the crock and then top with ordinary compost, having 2cm (1in) of the sieved soil on top.

Small seeds must not be buried, but larger ones can be just pressed into the soil. Water the first time by standing in containers of water so that the whole soil can be well moistened. Place in the frame with a piece of glass on top and then cover with dark paper. The best time to sow is in early spring in a temperature of 21°C (70°F); seeds will germinate at a lower temperature, but take longer to do so. Once seedlings appear the paper should be removed and the glass raised slightly. Keep them away from direct sunshine for the first year but make sure they have plenty of light or they will become drawn. Never let seed pots dry out while germination is taking place. Watering may be done with a fine spray.

Prick out when the cotyledon has been absorbed. Before this the root is so tiny that it can be broken very easily, killing the seedling. The seedlings may be placed 2·5cm (1in) apart in a cactus compost in boxes made of concrete or plastic until they are ready to go into 5cm (2in) pots. Be careful not to put them into pots too soon, as these dry out very quickly.

Cacti and succulents come in all shapes and sizes. Above left is Cotyledon Paraguayense, with its silvery green rosettes. Above right is the grotesque form of Opuntia microdasys cristata. Below left is the delicate starry flower of Glottiphyllum darisii.

VEGETABLES, FRUIT AND HERBS

Fruit, vegetables and herbs can all be grown on a very small scale, whether you have a garden or not. Even root vegetables such as beetroot or potatoes can be grown in large pots or tubs and broad beans, (left), look decorative during their flowering period.

YOU DO NOT necessarily need an orchard to grow an apple, a vegetable plot to grow a bean or a herb garden to grow mint.

Many fruits, vegetables, and herbs can be grown in unusual as well as confined or limited spaces. It is a matter of selecting the right varieties for the conditions you can provide.

Small-scale fruit cultivation

You can have your own fruit even in a town flat or house if it has only a balcony or windowsill big enough to accommodate a large pot, and sunny enough for fruit to ripen. Nectarines, peaches, apples, pears, grapes, figs, cherries, almonds and quinces are perfectly at home against a sheltered wall on a patio or terrace, either in a container or directly into the ground, with the paving coming close to the growing trunk, leaving just enough space for watering. Restricting the roots of many fruit trees encourages them to spend their energy producing fruit, rather than excess wood and leaf. Citrus fruit can be grown outdoors too in sheltered places, but will not produce edible fruit and must be looked on as ornaments.

Nurserymen are producing more fruit trees and bushes on dwarf-like root stock. Apart from keeping to the individual pruning schedules, fruit trees in restricted places are no more difficult to grow than Christmas trees or hydrangeas.

The best trees for potting are stocky ones with short trunks, which makes them less liable to be blown over. You will need a box or pot or other container at least 60cm (2ft) square or in

Fruit trees can be grown in very little space if they are trained to grow against walls. This apple tree is grown on the triple cordon system, and provides a plentiful crop as well as disguising a dull blank wall. Peach and apricot trees respond well to this treatment as well, and really enjoy the shelter and warmth of a south-facing wall.

diameter and the same measurement deep, with drainage holes. Put broken crocks in the bottom, then a layer of good rich soil. Spread out the roots of the tree, and gradually put in the rest of the soil, shaking the main trunk gently at times to make sure there are no air pockets around the fine feeding roots; then firm the soil gently. Hold the tree in position so that the soil reaches the same level at which it grew in the nursery.

The trees should not need feeding until the fruit has set, and after this they need a weekly feed of liquid manure until the crop is gathered. Established trees should have the top few centimetres (inches) of soil gently removed and replaced with fresh compost in autumn or spring. Some trees remain in the same pots for 20 years and more, with an occasional wash and brush up below ground.

If the tree seems to be declining and the crop sparse, lay the pot on its side and spray the soil from the roots with a hose, so as not to damage them. Cut back any large thick roots without damaging the fine, hairy ones. Put the tree back in the same container and add new compost. Do not be tempted to put it into a larger container, or it will make more growth, at the expense of fruit, and eventually cease to be a dwarf. Figs do particularly well in pots, because they get the root restriction and good drainage which are essential to them. They thrive outdoors in sun during their growing season, but next year's figs will only mature if the shoots can be kept free of frost in the winter. This is no problem with portable containers, as the plants can be moved out of danger, once the leaves have fallen, to an entrance hall, sunroom or porch—anywhere airy and light. It does not have to be warm, only frost-proof.

Smaller pots and containers can usually be heaved manually into different, more felicitous positions when necessary. Large, heavy pots and containers are another matter when you have to get them hurriedly out of a gale or snow storm. However, wooden containers can easily be fixed with castors before they are planted, and pots could

Below: Orange trees can be grown in pots, but without quite a lot of heat you cannot expect them to fruit very satisfactorily. Below left: Many fruit trees have been specially developed to grow in a confined space. This is 'Laxton's Fortune', an early ripening variety which is a heavy cropper, and the fruit is remarkably resistant to scab.

It is surprising how many vegetables can be grown in pots— in fact some of the more exotic kinds like aubergines (or eggplants) and capsicums (sweet peppers) seem to thrive in them. Careful attention to water and plant food, as well as a place in the sun, will insure quite substantial yields. In this back yard (right) there is a typical collection, including climbing French beans and tomatoes at the back, capsicum (centre left), and left to right in the front, parsley, dwarf French (stick) beans, celery and aubergine (eggplant).

be placed on little trollies, smaller than their bases, so they cannot be seen.

Space should not prevent anyone from growing a few unusual soft fruits: red and white currants as well as the more common black; boysenberries, thornless loganberries, dessert gooseberries, yellow raspberries, perpetual fruiting Zeva raspberries, and blueberries if you give them an acid compost. All of these, whether bushes or climbers can be grown in pots on patios or balconies, as long as there is sufficient sun. Climbers can be trained on boundary fences, or up trellis with their roots in containers or the open soil. Alpine and perpetual strawberries will grow in window boxes, and any kind of container, including special 'strawberry barrels' with planting holes drilled round their sides, and they also make attractive path edgings.

Having fruit very much under your eye will mean there is much less bird pilfering than in a quiet, remote garden. If you do need to protect the fruit, use fine mesh netting. The only disadvantage of growing fruit in containers, particularly soft varieties, is that they must never be allowed to dry out, so make sure someone reliable is lined up to water them if you are away from home. Even a weekend without water could do irreparable damage.

Pruning varies considerably with the different cane and soft fruits, and with bush and tree fruits, will depend on what ultimate shape you want to achieve. The treatment of espaliers and cordons against walls or wires is quite different from that of bush or dwarf standard fruit trees. There are many inexpensive, illustrated booklets on pruning which are simple to follow.

Small-scale vegetable growing
Vegetables will grow in the most unlikely containers, and places, as long as you provide them with soil, compost or some form of sustenance. Containers can be large or small, decorative or humdrum—urns, tin cans, buckets, fruit baskets, window boxes, sinks— anything so long as there is enough

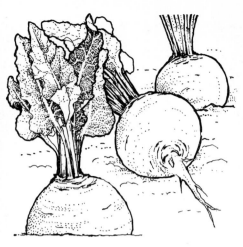

Right: Start sweetcorn off in individual pots before planting in a compact square outside. They must be close together, as it is essential for cross-pollinization. Far right: Beetroot grows well in a small vegetable patch, in tubs or pots, or alternatively plant it in a flower bed where its attractive foliage blends well with flowering plants. Below: This climbing frame for marrows or squash is really simple to construct from offcuts of wood. Opposite: Climbing beans (runner, climbing French, wax or purple-podded) grow well in pots or tubs. Construct a 'wigwam' of string or canes for them to cling to.

depth for their various root sizes.

Bush marrow and squashes will grow happily in containers in a sunny yard or balcony, and the climbing varieties of these and cucumbers make splendid outdoor wall decorations. Courgettes (or zucchini) and custard marrows, cut in their infancy with the flowerhead barely fading, are the most delicious and prolific of any summer vegetable.

Other edible wall and fence decorations are trailing and climbing vegetables such as stringless climbing French beans, purple podded and golden wax beans, all vastly superior in flavour and behaviour to the old red flowered runner bean, although this is certainly still one of the favourite types. Grow it in large tubs trained up a 'wigwam' of bamboo canes—six to eight plants would grow happily in a tub or pot 30cm (12in) across. For path edgings use dwarf French and broad beans (the latter have beautifully scented flowers), early stump rooted carrots, or golden, white and red beetroot whose leaves are as attractive as many flowers. Small fruiting bush tomatoes look unexpectedly decorative dotted among flowers in an open bed, or against walls. They are also easy to grow in pots and do not require any support.

Jerusalem artichokes take up very little space and can be used as a windbreak, a sunshade, or a summer screen to shut out the neighbours. A thicket of them can be better than a fence. They are not in the least fussy about soil, grow 1·5m to 2m (5 to 6ft) tall, need no attention, and the roots can be stored or dug up and eaten when you want them in winter.

Corn (or maize), can also be used as a summer screen, but never in a single row. It must be planted in a tight block, so that the male plume at the top of each plant can fertilize the silken tassels of the pods below. They take up surprisingly little space.

Lettuce, radishes and spring onions can all be grown in window boxes or pots on the window sill as long as you do not mind them spoiling the view!

With limited space, potatoes may seem an extreme way of squandering it. However, to some people, new potatoes at Christmas taste even better than caviare, if they are home grown! Save or buy early lifted crops (green ones are perfectly all right). Put them in a light place to make shoots. In July or August, remove all but three of the 'eyes', plant them in pots or half barrels and keep them in a dark sheltered place until the shoots come through the soil. They can be put into an open garage or shed if it is not too cool, and then brought into the house, or some other source of gentle warmth until they have produced and let drop their insignificant flowers. They must be kept watered, but not overfed.

Growing in bags

The easiest and most versatile way of growing something to eat in limited spaces is in the new large growing bags. The drawback is that they are both ugly and expensive. However, the first fault can be mitigated by careful disguise.

Nothing can help with the price except to make the most possible use of each bag.

The average bag contains about 15kg (35lb) of nutrient-enriched compost, is about 1m (39in) long by 40cm (15in) wide and 15cm (6in) deep. If you are investing in several bags, when you lay them out leave at least 40cm (15in) between their ends and 22cm (9in) between double rows. Basic instructions are included in every bag, or printed on it.

These bags can be used anywhere except cool and shady places—against a south-facing house wall, in a conservatory or house extension, in a greenhouse, along a path, on a patio or in a sheltered garden. Never sow seeds directly into a bag, but use ready-raised plants. In this way a wide range of vegetables can spring from these practically fool-proof containers. You can grow in them plants which would normally be considered only for greenhouses, such as sweet peppers, tomatoes, cucumbers, melons, aubergines (or eggplants). Runner beans can be grown successfully, and are an exception in that they may be grown from seed put directly into the opened bag.

There are several ways of supporting climbing plants such as runner beans and tomatoes, but on no account must the bottom of the bag be pierced with canes. Stout stakes can be driven into the ground at either end of the bags, and wires or string stretched between to which are attached supporting canes. Where the bags are on a solid, soilless base, put up a trellis or stiff, plastic-covered wire mesh behind them to support the plants, or put vine hooks into the wall with wires between, to take canes or string. Another way is to put stout cord or wire right under the bags at intervals, and stretch the double ends above as high as you want, attached to the wall behind. Use whichever suits the growing habits of particular plants best, depending on the position of the bags.

Each bag will hold three to four tomato plants, depending on whether you let them make five or more trusses; three aubergines or peppers; two marrows, six strawberries, ten runner beans or two cucumbers. This is just a guide, as there is no limit to the variety of plants you can grow in them, including salads and herbs: it is simply a matter of counting the cost. If you have even a small amount of open ground, it would be uneconomic to waste an expensive bag on radishes and lettuces which can usually be bought cheaply. However, to those with only a concrete patio, or balcony, and who are keen on readily available fresh salad vegetables, it could be well worth the cost. Lettuce is the one crop which, because of its short growing period, may be grown in the same bag again after the first crop is cleared, provided some liquid feeding is carried out. With two or more bags you could have a succession of lettuce so there would be no gap between crops.

There is no straightforward answer to how much watering plants grown in these bags will need. Initially, each bag should be given about 8 litres (2 gallons) of water immediately after planting. Subsequently, the amount will vary according to temperature, weather conditions and the vigour of the plants. If a little care is taken, no drainage holes are necessary. Never over-water so that the compost at the bottom is standing in a puddle, or the roots will rot. During vigorous growth and hot spells, a fair quantity of water is needed. However it is best *not* to make drainage holes as these would make it more difficult to rewet a dry bag. If, by accident, a bag does become waterlogged and holes are essential, make them at the ends or along the sides just above soil level, to minimize the risk of contaminating the compost.

A bag should never be allowed to dry right out. However, should this happen, 10 litres (2½ gallons) will be needed to bring it back to normal. This is easier to do where drainage holes have *not* been made in the bag.

Do not attempt to store the bag at the end of the season, and use it for the same crop next year—it is not worth the risk.

Propagating bags are the latest innovation in small scale vegetable gardening. They are expensive of course, and can only be used for one season, but their special formula of nutrient-enriched compost does produce fantastic yields from plants like tomatoes, aubergines (eggplants), courgettes (zucchini) or peppers.

(This does not apply to perennial herbs grown in bags.) Dig the compost into your garden, if you have one, or give it to someone who has. It will be most welcome.

If for some reason you have bought bags which you have been unable to use, they will remain in good condition for two seasons as long as they are *unopened*, and are kept reasonably cool; never expose them to direct heat or sunshine when in storage.

Planting in a small area

When planting crops in a small area, it often pays to ignore accepted rules about distances apart between seeds, plants and rows. Use the rule of thumb and some imagination. Results have proved that many crops like to be huddled together. It means that you cannot get the hoe easily among them, but the closeness helps to keep out weeds and in dry weather keeps the ground shaded. There is no need to stick to rigid rows for quick growing crops either. Forget about thinning out seedlings too, until they are really crowding one another. Most instructions are for perfectionists who want the biggest and the best.

With crops such as beet, carrots, turnips, kohlrabi and spring onions, sow thickly in a wide drill, and start to thin them when they are just large enough to eat. Firm the soil afterwards so the others can continue to grow properly. The cook may find it a fiddly business to prepare them, but they are much tastier than the larger, later ones. Some crops have to be grown cheek to cheek, such as self-blanching celery. Peas too, do better when sown thickly in a broad drill, the rows only wide enough for your feet when picking them. There is no need to stake the dwarf varieties, they produce more pods by flopping against each other and keeping the ground cool. Do not attempt to weed them once they have germinated or you will disturb the roots. The crop will be over before the weeds can do any harm, and the ground put to rights then. To save space, crops can be grown in blocks instead of single rows, and salad seeds scattered in any odd bare patch as long as there is sun.

A most valuable and unusual bean is Fiskeby V, higher in protein and other nutrients than practically any other food, including prime steak and milk. Because of its upright habit it likes to be grown close together, with at most

There are various space-saving techniques for a small vegetable patch. Below right: Intercropping means planting fast-maturing crops between rows of slower-growing ones; here lettuces are grown between runner bean rows: the lettuces will be harvested before the beans take all the light from them. Below: Lettuce is being grown on the ridges of celery trenches.

7cm (3in) between the plants, which only reach a height of about 30cm (12in), on single stems. The beans form in small hairy pods which are picked when about 2cm (1½in) long and cooked in their shells, which then slip off easily. They are delicious green but can be left till autumn to use as miniature haricots. A most valuable space-saver.

Another unusual vegetable which takes very little room and is pretty enough to grow among the flowers is the asparagus pea, which is very difficult to find in the shops.

It has pretty red flowers and grows to about 45cm (18in) with no need of stakes. It is not a true pea: the flowers turn into winged pods which must be picked when 1·5cm (1in) long or they will be inedibly stringy. They are delicious steamed whole and served with melted butter. But you have to keep a constant eye on them, as the pods have the trick of turning from infancy to old age almost overnight. Fresh flowers form prolifically which shield the forming pods from obvious view so daily inspection is necessary. Pick even those which have escaped you till they are too brittle to eat, for if you leave them on, the plants will stop flowering and concentrate on ripening the seeds.

Another way of making the most of a small space is to use the method of cultivation called intercropping. You grow a quick maturing crop close to one which takes longer, such as summer spinach, lettuce and radish between rows of peas; or salad crops between potatoes. Use them as soon as possible, and the main crops can grow on undisturbed.

Catch-cropping serves a similar pur-pose. You grow fast-maturing crops on ground which is later to be used for something more important. Sow radishes in spring, where outdoor tomatoes will be planted when frosts are over; lettuce where celery and winter greens are to be; Chinese cabbage to grow quickly in the space vacated by early potatoes. With this kind of intensive growing you will need to keep the ground well fed and watered.

Vegetables indoors

If you have not a place outside sunny and sheltered enough for growing green peppers, try them indoors on a window ledge in individual, ordinary flower pots. Started off early in the season and kept well watered and occasionally fed, they crop remarkably well and look most attractive.

You can also keep up a constant supply of sprouting seeds indoors, for salads and cooking. Though of more value in winter when salad crops are most expensive, they fill the inevitable gap in supplies, and add an interesting textural contrast, as well as exotic flavour, to any kind of salad. The best known is probably the mung bean, but there are others more interesting—alfalfa, fenugreek, aduki, triticale—or they can be bought as a mixture. There are various ways of growing them without going to the expense of a special 'sprouter'. They can be spread on a saucer or dish on flannel or blotting paper, and kept damp (and dark if you want the shoots blanched), in a temperature which reaches 19°C (65°F) or more during the day. They should have sprouted enough to eat between three and five days (the warmer the quicker). The trouble with this method is that it limits you to a certain quantity, and the crop usually has to be cut to harvest, which inevitably wastes some of it.

One of the best and cheapest method of keeping up a continuous supply is by using glass fruit juice jars, with a piece of muslin or cheesecloth over the top held in place with a rubber band. Rinse the estimated amount of seed for the size of your jar (usually three or four level tablespoons), put it into the jar, and half fill with tepid water. Cover the top with muslin or cheesecloth which allows water in and out easily, and fix with a rubber band. Shake vigorously and drain off the water. Lay the jar on its side in a temperature between 13°C (55°F) and 19°C (65°F). Repeat this process morning and evening until the sprouts are ready (two to eight days depending on variety and warmth).

Detailed instructions are usually given for the different varieties when you buy them from specialist seedsmen, but certain growing points must be kept in mind. Never put the jar or container directly on a radiator, or anything which produces considerable heat. Use tepid or cold water for rinsing, *never* hot. The seeds can be put in a higher temperature to start them sprouting,

but for only a short period. The muslin will change colour as the seed casing dissolves into the rinsing water. If the sprouting seeds smell less than fresh, rinse more often, or grow them in cooler conditions. Discard any seeds which have not sprouted after six days.

Growing herbs

If you have a garden, the obvious place to grow herbs is as close to the kitchen as possible. However, whether you have a garden or not, herbs can conveniently be grown in pots, window boxes or tubs to give a supply of fresh herbs all the year round.

Some herbs can be grown even closer to hand in individual pots, or grouped together in containers on the window-sill of a sunny kitchen. Those which will survive and even enjoy this position include chives, parsley, thyme, and annuals such as basil, sweet marjoram, chervil and dill.

Keep them moist but not over-watered, with the exception of basil, which goes weak at the knees and dies off unless kept on the dry side.

Larger perennial herbs like tarragon, lovage, fennel, sage, bay and rosemary all make interesting container plants, particularly the evergreen bay, sage and rosemary.

The wide variety of thymes are perfect for growing in window boxes, for their appearance, flower scent and culinary uses. They do have to be trimmed back after they have flowered, to keep them from becoming 'leggy' and unsightly, but only as far as last year's growth, not into it, or the plant will die.

If all of us had started with mint in containers rather than open ground there would be better tempers and less backache for those who have to dig its invasive roots from more treasured and permanent plants such as globe artichokes, asparagus and cane fruit. Mint cannot be recommended for decoration throughout the year, as it dies down in winter. But some of the variegated and purple leaved varieties look delightful throughout the summer. A portable container would be best, rather than a

Below: Growing bean-sprouts at home in a jar. The beans are placed in a jam jar with muslin fixed over it, and warm water is inserted, shaken and then discarded every day for about a week. (See text for full details.)

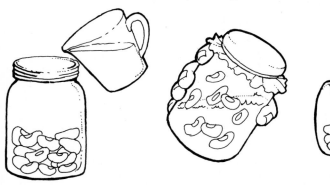

An effective herb garden can be constructed like a large window box with separate compartments for the various types of herb.

93

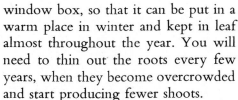

Some of the useful culinary and aromatic herbs which are easy to grow in pots or window boxes. Above: Lemon balm, Melissa officinalis. Above right: The attractive flowers of chives. Right: Bay, Laurus nobilis. Far right: A variegated form of sage. Below: Parsley can be grown indoors in a pottery jar, which looks attractive as well as being useful.

window box, so that it can be put in a warm place in winter and kept in leaf almost throughout the year. You will need to thin out the roots every few years, when they become overcrowded and start producing fewer shoots.

For a permanent planting of herbs in a window box a good choice would be sage, lemon thyme, rosemary and bay. Parsley could be added to these for a short stay but as it is a very slow growing biennial it would have to be replaced after eighteen months. By continually nipping pieces off container herbs, you will automatically control their size and keep them producing new growth.

All the annuals can easily be raised in the house from seed. With a little ingenuity, you can keep up a supply throughout the year by using mini-cloches, or an ordinary flower pot covered by a polythene bag, to germinate the seeds. Sow the seeds thinly in ordinary soil or potting compost, barely covering them. Put on the cloche lids or polythene bags secured upside-down round the rim by a rubber band, leaving a few inches of breathing space. Put the pots in a warm dark place, such as an airing cupboard, until the seeds germinate, then bring them into the light and take off the covers when the seedlings are about 15mm ($\frac{1}{2}$in) tall. Pull out and discard weak seedlings if germination has been so successful that the pots will become overcrowded. Any light place will do for the remaining seedlings and room temperature will suit them. A sunny spot is not essential, but if that is all you have to offer, keep a careful watch on the soil to make sure they never dry out. Be prepared to move them around to cooler or warmer conditions if they seem unhappy. What suits one herb, may not suit another. My basil, for instance, is always particularly happy in the bathroom!

In general, most herbs out of doors like a sunny, warm place with well drained soil, not too heavy, but which does not dry out quickly. They can be grown along paths among flowers, in bags, deep or shallow sinks, according to how much depth their individual roots need, or in a patch of ground all to themselves, making sure the taller ones do not rob the short ones of sun. Some roots of those from the garden can be lifted and put in pots or boxes in late autumn, and put in a frost-free place to provide fresh leaves during winter. This could be in a light garage or shed, but do not forget them! They will need watering and may want a change of scene or air. Parsley, and perennials which die down or lose their leaves in hard weather, are the ones to pot up. Among the most useful are tarragon, pot marjoram, chives, French sorrel, fennel and chervil.

Drying herbs

There is often a wastage of home-grown herbs because they are harvested and dried wrongly. They can be dried, either on racks in an airy, dry shed or room, hung in small bunches in a warm draught or laid on racks in a oven which is turned off, but is still warm from previous use. Then rub them to fine particles and store in airtight jars. Their flavour is destroyed by light so the jars should either be light-proof or stored in a dark place. Every herb grower has a pet method, and each herb reacts differently to various methods. It is very much a question of trial and error, and can depend on what the growing season has been like or the weather conditions when they are harvested. If you find mint turns brown in the oven, try picking it on a dry day, shake it well to get rid of insects and dust, and put it head down in a brown paper bag in the sun till crisp. Then store it. Or you can make fresh mint into a sauce as if you were going to use it at once. Chop the leaves, add sugar, pour on boiling vinegar, allow to cool, then pour into bottles and cover. Make sure the corks or screw tops have a layer of vinegar-proof paper inside them to avoid evaporation.

Choose a dry, still day to harvest other herbs after early morning dew has dried but before the sun gets hot. The cutting time of the incomparable sweet marjoram is vital—in the two months of high summer just as the buds are about to open, leaving 5cm (2in) of stem and leaf for a second crop.

Herbs can be stored in a freezer, either chopped and packed into ice cube containers then turned out into bags, or whole in plastic bags. Herbs and treatment vary enormously and it is better to consult a book on home freezing if you are going to store them in this way.

The best way of preserving herbs is to dry them. Store them in air-tight jars in a dark place.

CARE AND CULTIVATION

THE MOST important factor when bringing up indoor or container plants, whether grown from seed yourself or 'adopted', is to discover their individual needs. No two plants behave alike, even in the same environment: they are individualists.

Any type of restricted gardening is basically unnatural and plants grown in these conditions generally need more careful attention than those in the open garden. Whether they are in the house, on balconies or patios, in window boxes, baskets, tubs or troughs, their water, soil and air conditions cannot be left to nature. The roots will not grow unless the soil suits them and leaves will not develop unless the air is to their liking.

It is up to you to decide whether you choose the plants first and then find a place to suit them; or whether there is an awkward position you want to fill with plants which have to be restricted to the types which will survive there.

A healthy plant, bought from a reliable nursery, should be able to look after itself for the first few months with no extra feeding, just the required amount of water. There are dangers, however, in transferring plants from the light, humid atmosphere of a greenhouse to the drier and usually less light conditions of a living room, even when the temperature is about the same. The plants find it easier to adjust when they are bought in the spring and summer, and can adapt to their new environment before central or other artificial heating has to be used, making the air additionally dry. Leaves may yellow and fall off during the first few days, but the plants will soon accustom themselves to their new station in life provided they are not overwatered, are given fresh air *out* of a draught and are in good light, but not direct sun. There are pot plants to suit most extremes of luxury or deprivation which can be found in and out of doors and the choice of houseplants will depend very much on light. In general most flowering pot plants and alpines want full light, bromeliads and palms can take it in half measures, and ferns, and deep, dark green plants will tolerate quite dim conditions. (See plant list).

General care of plants indoors

Here are some points to remember with house and semi-indoor plants, whether in individual pots, miniature gardens or containers.

1. However light and sunny a room appears to us, it is far less so than in the open garden, under the sky, even in a slightly shaded place. If you have a photographic light meter, try comparing the reading in your living room with that in semi-shade outdoors. There will be a marked difference.

2. Never change plants' growing positions too violently, such as suddenly putting a newly planted hanging basket that has been nurtured in a light, sheltered place, against a sunny front door at the mercy of breezes; or taking a portable miniature garden, languishing from indoor life, straight out into the sunniest part of the garden. It will suffer the equivalent of sunstroke. Each transition, whether in the growing-up stages of being re-potted and pruned, or having to change homes in later life, must be in slow motion. Plants do not have much resilience to violent change.

3. In winter, remove window-ledge plants before drawing curtains. They can suffer from draught, frostbite, or early morning scorching by the sun.

4. Damp the foliage of alpines with a fine spray, using tepid water and a pinch of wetting compound in hot weather, once a day. Only 'mist' them, do not saturate. This washes off the dust so that the leaves can breathe and also discourages red spider mite which breeds at a rollicking pace in hot, dry conditions.

5. Many plants will not tolerate the fumes from coke or oil burners. However, gas is usually inoffensive from modern equipment, if the installation is properly maintained.

Watering indoors

Watering should always be with rain water if possible, as it contains oxygen. Let it stand in a can or bucket before use, at the same temperature as the plants to be watered, so as not to chill the roots.

More container plants die from over watering than from drought. Young plants and those growing fast or in full bloom need more than those which are resting or than older, mature plants. There is no set pattern for watering but there are at least some methods to be avoided. A regular trickle a day does more harm than good. It is nearly always better to water infrequently, but thoroughly. If more water is given than the plant needs, the roots begin to rot as they can no longer fulfil their function of taking up water. The same symptoms show when there is not enough water— the leaves go limp, yellow and brown, and flowers wither and fall off. The only solution to waterlogging is to take the plant from its pot, remove the sodden earth and cut off all dead brown and black roots (healthy ones are white or yellow), then put back into fresh soil, and cut the plant back a little so the reduced roots do not have too much work to do while they recover.

Many plants like a good soak at about weekly intervals. Put individual pot plants in a bowl of water up to the rim of the pot and leave until little air bubbles stop rising to the surface. This may take only a few minutes, or at the most half an hour. Let the pots drain thoroughly before returning to a saucer or container. This method also helps to revive plants such as hydrangeas, primulas and cyclamen, whose soil has completely dried out.

Never let them stand in the surplus water or the roots will drown. Plants growing in soilless compost should not be allowed to dry out completely. They must be kept damper than those in ordinary potting soil.

Whether the plants are inside or out, a few simple rules for watering should keep them, and you, out of trouble.

1. Never water when the surface soil is damp.

2. Never let any plants stand in a puddle.

3. Never let water float on the top surface for more than a few seconds, for this means that the top soil has become panned, or caked, forming a crust which will not let the water penetrate. Even if it eventually soaks through, it will not have been able to take any essential air with it. Scratch up the surface about an inch deep, according to the size of the container, so that both water and air can pass freely to the roots.

4. Water indoor plants less in winter than summer, for, although the room temperature may be the same, there will be less light, so that leaves will not need as much moisture, nor the roots as much carbon dioxide.

5. In hot weather outside plants in particular should be watered in early morning or early evening, and in particularly hot weather, both. Do not water them when the sun is on them— hot sun on wet foliage can cause scorching.

Feeding

Feeding is of prime importance. In natural conditions plants sink their roots and send them scouting for water and nutrients, which will vary according to locality, depending on soil type and conditions.

Obviously, plants living a restricted life will need a specially good soil, adjusted for their particular taste to maintain them over a long period. Fortunately this is simple today. The chemical

To turn out a plant from a pot, take it in the hand with the fingers spread over the soil surface and upturn the pot. Strike the rim sharply on a firm surface, and the pot can then be lifted clear of the ball of soil.

industry offers a great many compound fertilizers containing the various salt nutrients with all the trace elements in the correct proportions. These can be bought in liquid form or as soluble powder. Whichever you choose, make sure the manufacturer has given full details of the formula, and adequate instructions as to strength and frequency of application. Never try to be clever by adding a little extra for luck, or a little less if you are feeling mean. In the first case you may cause irreparable damage, and in the second, you are wasting money as you will have to revert more quickly to the correct quantity.

Chemical firms spend a great deal of time and money researching each product before it is put on sale to the ordinary gardener and considered safe and foolproof. If anything goes wrong, you have probably misread the directions.

There are special 'personalized' compounds for highly sensitive, individual types of plants like cacti, bromeliads, orchids and azaleas. However, an ordinary compound fertilizer is all that is needed for the majority of container and miniature garden plants.

Sink or trough gardens, planted in good soil at the start, can often go for two or three years without extra food, depending on what you are growing. With good drainage, so that the soil cannot become sour, some can go well beyond ten years with nothing more than an occasional top dressing of a proprietary potting compost, appropriate to the occupants. Alpines and conifers in particular growing in sinks, troughs or shallower containers such as dish gardens, should have very sparse helpings of fertilizer or they will make unnaturally lush growth and lose their characteristic compactness, as well as their strength and dignity. This is especially true of bonsai trees which need very carefully controlled feeding.

What a plant requires in the way of food varies as to type, size, development, age and size of container. Generally plants rest in winter and need less, but more as the days become warmer. Never give liquid fertilizer to a plant with dried-out soil. Water it well first, or if it is in a pot, soak it in tepid water for half an hour and feed a few days later when it has recovered.

Pests and diseases

Plant diseases are always a warning signal that something is wrong with the way the plant is being cultivated, whether the damage is caused by bacteria, virus, fungi or insects. Well grown plants, in the correct position, can withstand these attacks without help or visible signs of damage.

When it is obvious that a plant is sick, besides treating the visible symptoms, look for the underlying causes. Is it in the wrong temperature or a draught? Has it enough light? Is the soil exhausted? Is it too dry or too damp? Work your way through these before looking for pests or fungi, although these can be encouraged by poor conditions.

If the main part of the plant is severely diseased, it is best to get rid of

Right: Aphids can be winged or wingless. They cluster on the stems and under the leaves of plants, and suck the sap. The black variety play particular havoc with broad beans and nasturtiums in the early growing period, so check frequently for signs of infestation.

the whole thing, particularly if it is easy to replace. But in the case of what should be a long-lived favourite, take cuttings from the healthy parts before you finally part with it.

The most common pests likely to attack indoor and outdoor container plants are aphids, red spider mite, scale insects, white fly and mealybug. The main diseases are mildew, greymould and 'damping off'.

Aphids These include green and black-fly. They cluster on the undersides of young leaves and on the tender tips of shoots and flower buds to feed on the plant's sap. *Cure:* Spray with an insecticide. There are also systemic insecticides which are absorbed into the plant through the roots, and insects sucking the sap are destroyed. The advantage of these over spraying is that the insecticide does not have to be directly aimed at the insects. Spraying is often awkward as aphids especially are usually on the underside of leaves.

Red spider mite Not easy to recognize as it is so minute. It can only be seen by sharp eyes, or with a magnifying glass. The first signs of danger are fine webs on the underside of leaves, which then develop yellowish patches and drop off. *Cure:* Use malathion or kelthane.

White fly Winged insects about 1–2mm ($\frac{1}{16}$in) long, white, triangular and found on the underside of leaves, which dart off as soon as the leaves are moved. The larvae are protected by tiny shells. *Cure:* Repeated attacks with malathion.

Scale insects Brownish insects looking like minute mussel shells. They remain in stationary clusters on the foliage and stems, sucking up the sap; the leaves then turn dingy with patches of sooty mould. *Cure:* Treat with systemic insecticide or spray with liquid malathion.

Mealy bug Troublesome and mobile insects about 2–3mm ($\frac{1}{12}$in) long, rather like white woodlice with a fine white cottony covering of waxy threads. Usually found in the leaf axils and under young leaves, feeding on the sap. *Cure:* Spray with malathion or use a

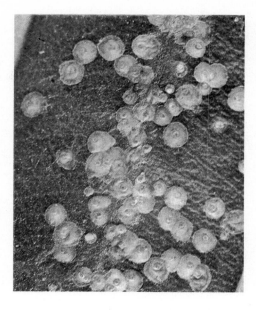

Left: Oleander scale also attacks many many plants from aucuba to cyclamen. Look for them on leaves and stems.

systemic insecticide.

Mildew Round, whitish patches appear on leaves, stems, buds and flowers, followed by a floury grey deposit which covers the whole plant. *Cure:* A systemic fungicide, or a copper fungicide spray.

Grey mould (Botrytis) A grey furry covering which at first grows on only the dead parts of a plant, but will soon attack the living parts too if the atmosphere is too damp, the plants are too close together, or there is not enough light and warmth. *Cure:* Remove and burn all affected parts, then

Below: Mildew's unsightly marking is easy to recognize; here, it has attacked the leaves of a rose.

Many plants can be propagated by leaf cuttings. Top: A healthy leaf is pegged flat on sandy compost and the main vein is slit. Centre: New plants grow where the slits were made. Above: The individual plants can now be potted up.

dust with a fungicide.

Damping off This may attack the stems of seedlings and cuttings, which collapse and die. *Cure:* Use a hormone rooting powder containing captan when taking cuttings. Use a combined seed dressing before sowing. Water the soil afterwards or spray with liquid captan or copper fungicide in place of plain water. Or use orthocize dust.

Propagation

There are many ways of starting or increasing your stock of plants for miniature gardens, without going to the expense of buying them. They can be grown from seed; cuttings can be taken from stem, leaf and root; or new plants can be formed from divisions, offsets and layering.

Seed A seed packet will usually give the basic information as to where, how and when the seeds should be sown. Do not be alarmed if a greenhouse is demanded. You can create the same conditions in miniature in the house, with the appropriate compost, plastic bags, or baby cloches. All can be found in garden shops, or improvised at no cost whatever. Sprinkle the seeds as thinly as possible on well-damped, soilless compost in pots or pans and place in a very light but sun-less spot. To create humidity, cover with polythene or glass but remove immediately germination can be seen. Then the seedlings must be given plenty of fresh air.

Stem cuttings For most plants this consists of taking vigorous young shoots, about 7·5cm (3in) long, with a short heel of mature wood cleanly cut at the base. With longer shoots, you need not go back to old wood, but cut just below a node from which the leaf buds spring. The leaves are then removed from the first node and the soft tip cut from the top, before the cutting is planted up usually into small pots or boxes of sandy, soilless compost.

Leaf cuttings This method is most suited to propagate soft and fleshy leaves. Use well developed leaves, nick or score the main rib on the underside, and then lay the leaf flat on the soil.

African violets are particularly happy to be propagated in this way in a mixture of sand and peat.

Division Some plants produce young shoots at their base at certain stages of their growth. These can be removed and potted up individually. If the mother plant is in a pot, knock it out and gently tease the soil away, and with a sharp knife, cut off the new shoots with some of the closest roots attached to them.

Layering Any low growing branches of a shrub or perennial plant can be bent till it touches the soil. Make a nick beneath the bark to keep it in contact with the soil and also encourage new growth and pin it down with a clothes peg, wire or a stone. New roots will start to form, and when the young plant is obviously living a life of its own it can be separated from the parent. This method is more suited to outdoor plants where they are not to be a decoration constantly under scrutiny.

Propagation is of necessity a complex and individual matter in the plant world, to which whole books are devoted. These are general guides, limited by space.

Tools for small plants

Watering can with a fine rose easily removed for cleaning.
A syringe for damping foliage.
A different and labeled syringe for using chemicals.
Small trowel and fork (kitchen discards will do).
Forceps or eyebrow tweezers for removing small weeds.
Small paintbrush for removing dust and soil from low-growing plants when there has been replanting or potting.

General care

Constantly remove the dead heads from flowering plants.
Stake plants which need it as discreetly as possible.
Prune or pinch back plants to your own wishes, if they can stand it; never be bullied by them.

A PLANT LIST

This plant list is meant as a guide to the sorts of plants and flowers which can be grown in certain situations and makes no claim to be comprehensive! Many of the plants and flowers given can be used for other purposes than those given—it will be up to you to experiment with the best combinations. Very specialized plants such as those required for bonsai or bottle gardens are given in the relevant chapters, as well as further suggestions for more ordinary containers and for sink gardens.

Bulbs for tubs and windowboxes

Winter Aconite (Eranthis)
Species: *E. Lyemalis* (var. *cilicica*, *sibirica*)

Crocus
Species: There are many, in colours varying from white, yellow, lilac and purple. *C. vernus*, *C. chrysanthus* and *C. versicolor* are all interesting.

Autumn Crocus (Colchicum)
Species: *C. agrippinum*, *C. autumnale* 'Meadow Saffron', *C. decaisnei*, var. *album*, *C. variegatum*

Glory of the Snow (Chionodoxa)
Species: *C. cretica*, *C. luciliae*, *C. sardensis*

Grape Hyacinth (Muscari)
Species: *M. botryoides*, var. *album*, *M. conicum*, *M. muscerinii*, 'Musk Hyacinth', *M. racemosum*, 'Starch Hyacinth'

Hyacinth (Hyacinthus)
Species: *H. orientalis*, 'Common Hyacinth', var. *albulus*, 'Roman Hyacinth'

Narcissus (Daffodil)
Species: Dwarf species are best, try *N. minimus*, 'Pygmy Daffodil', but there are many, many varieties to choose from in any garden suppliers'.

Scilla
Species: *S. amoena*, 'Star Hyacinth', *S. hispanica*, 'Spanish Squill', *S. siberica*, 'Siberian Squill'

Snowdrop (Galanthus)
Species: *G. nivalis*, 'Common Snowdrop'—there are many varieties of this, or *G. platyphyllus* and *G. carccasicus*, which are white and green.

Tulip (Tulipa)
Species: New varieties are developed every year and the choice in most garden suppliers' is bewildering. Any will grow in containers, but it is best to choose dwarf varieties in confined space.

Pot and bedding plants for tub gardening

Antirrhinum (Snapdragon)
Species: *A. majus*, and many garden varieties, including some useful dwarf varieties such as 'Tom Thumb'

Aucuba
Species: *A. japonica*, 'Spotted Laurel' and varieties

Begonia
Species: Some are grown for flower, others for foliage. There are many varieties so consult garden supplier. Colours vary from scarlet to rose and white.

Calceolaria (Slipper Flower)
Species: These can be herbaceous, shrubby or hardy—some are annuals, most garden suppliers have examples of each.

Calendula (Marigold)
Species: *C. officinalis*, with many varieties

Chrysanthemums and Marguerites
Species: Like pelargoniums there are numerous varieties but the compact pompons are best for container growing. Marguerites are in fact a species of Chrysanthemum—*C. frutescens*, as are *C. leucanthemum*, the Oxeye Daisy and *C. maximum*, the Shaster Daisy, both effective and hardy flowers for container growing.

Daisy (Bellis)
Species: Double daisies are delightful in container and miniature gardening. Most are varieties of *B.*

perennis flore-plens.

Fuchsia
Species: For container purposes the tender or half-hardy species rather than greenhouse species are best, for instance *F. magellanica*, and its varieties *conica, discolor, globosa* and *Riccartonii*. Greenhouse species can be put out in summer, but any frost will kill.

Geranium (Cranesbill)
Species: *G. Farreri, G. grandiflorum, G. Pylzowianum, G. tuberosum*

Hydrangea
Species: *H. macrophylla,* var. *Hortensia, Otaksa, H. petiolaris* (climbing), *H. arborescens grandiflora*

Lobelia
Species: *L. Erinus* and varieties

Pelargonium (Geranium)
Species: There are many many species and varieties of pelargonium, the best types for containers being zonal, ivy-leaved and scented-leaved, with many colours and many shapes and colours of leaves, some delightfully scented. A visit to a garden or houseplant supplier will help you choose.

Petunia
Species: *P. integrifolia, P. violecea,* and varieties from hybrids of these

Skimmia
Species: *S. Laureola, S. Reevesiana,* var. *rubella*

Sweet Alyssum (Lobularia)
Species: *L. maritima* (syn. *Alyssum maritimum*)

Tropaeolum (Nasturtium)
Species: *T. minus, T. majus* and varieties *nanum,* 'Tom Thumb Nasturtium'

Verbena (Vervain)
Species: *V. teucrioides*

Viola (Violet, Pansy)
Species: There are many species and varieties of show, fancy or tufted pansy and violettas, all of which are easy to grow, and which flower freely.

Zinnia (Youth-and-old-age)
Species: *Z. haageana, Z. linearis, Z. pauciflora*

Roses for miniature indoor gardens

Varieties: 'Baby Gold Star' (golden yellow); 'Cinderella' (white tinted carmine); 'Dwarf King' (velvet crimson); 'Little Flirt' (orange-red, yellow); 'New Penny' (salmon to pink); 'Pour Toi' (white semi-double); 'Rosina' (golden yellow); 'Tinker Bell' (bright pink).

For miniature gardens indoors or out

Anagallis (Pimpernel)
Species: *Anagallis tenella*

Arenaria (Sandwort)
Species: *Arenaria balearica*

Asperula
Species: *Asperula gussoni, A. suberosa*

Asplenium (Spleenwort)
Species: *A. ruta-muraria, A. Trichomanes*

Calceolaria
Species: *C. tenella*

Centaurium (Centaury)
Species: *C. portense* (syn. *Erythraea portense*)

Crassula
Species: *C. bolussi*

Erodium (Heron's Bill)
Species: *E. chamaedryoides* 'Roseum'

Helxine (Baby's Tears)
Species: *H. soleirolii,* 'Golden Queen', 'Silver Queen'

Hypericum (St John's Wort)
Species: *H. anagalloides*

Mentha (Mint)
Species: *M. requienii*

Rhodohypoxis
Species: *R. baurii, R. platypetala*

Scleranthus
Species: *Scleranthus biflorus*

Sedum (Stonecrop)
Species: *S. humifusum*

Selaginella
Species: *S. apada, S. helvetica,* var. 'Aurea'

Viola
Species: *Viola hederacea*

Wahlenbergia (Bell-flower)
Species: *W. tasmanica*

Trailing plants for hanging baskets and window boxes

Alyssum
Species: *A. saxatile,* 'Gold Dust'

Amaranthus (Love-lies-bleeding)
Species: *A. caudatus* (syns. *A. paniculatus* and *A. sanguineus*)

Aubrieta (Purple rock-cress)
Species: (Formerly spelt Aubretia) *A. deltoidea, A. granilis*

Begonia
Species: Pendulous varieties

Campanula
Species: *C. fragilis, C. garganica, C.*

garganica hirsuta, C. isophylla

Lobelia
Species: Trailing varieties

Lysimachia (Creeping Jenny)
Species: *L. mummularia*

Nemophila
Species: *N. maculata, N. Menziesii,*
'Baby Blue-eyes'

Nepeta
Species: *N. Cataria,* 'Catmint', *N.
Faaserii* (syn. *N. pseudemussinii*)

Pelargonium
Species: Ivy-leaved types

Periwinkle (Vinca)
Species: *V. major,* var. *variegata,
V. minus*

Petunia
See under *Pot and Bedding Plants*

Phacelia
Species: *P. campanularia, P. Parryi,
P. Whitlavia,* 'Californian Bluebell'

Phlox
Species: *P. adsurgens, P. nana, P.
subulata,* 'Moss Pink', and many
varieties

Tropaeolum (Nasturtium)
See *Pot and Bedding Plants*

Verbena (Vervain)
See *Pot and Bedding Plants*

Small-scale shrubs

Calluna
Species: *C. vulgaris,* 'Scotch
Heather', and many varieties

Cytisus (Broom)
Species: *C. Ardoinii, C. purpureus,*

C. decumbens, C. versicolor

Cotoneaster
Species: *C. microphylla*

Erica (Heath)
Species: *E. carnea, E. ciliaris* 'Dorset
Heath', *E. cinerea* 'Bell Heather',
E. darleyensis, E. Tetralix 'Cross-
leaved Heath' and many varieties

Euonymous (Spindle-tree)
Species: *E. radicans variegatus*

Genista
Species: *G. anglica, G. hispanica*
'Spanish Broom'

Helianthemum (Sun Rose)
Species: *H. nummularium* (syn. *H.
vulgare*), *H. Tuberaria* (syn. *Tuberaria
vulgaris*)

Juniper (Juniperus)
Species: *J. Sargentii, J. communis
compressa*

Santolina (Lavender Cotton)
Species: *S. Chamaecyparissus, S.
vireus* 'Holy Flax'

Fruit Trees and Bushes for Pots

Apple
Cox with James Grieveto to ensure
pollination; Charles Ross; Laxton's
Fortune
Apricots
Henstirk; Moorpark
Cherry
Bigarreau Napoleon with May
Duke; Early Rivers with Waterloo
Fig
White Marseilles
Nectarine
Early Rivers
Peach
Hale's Early; Duke of York; Royal
George
Pear
Doyenne du Comice with Clapp's

Favourite; Marie Louise
Plum
Coe's Golden Drop; Oulin's Gage
Jefferson

Dwarf Vegetables

Asparagus Pea
Aubergine
Broad Bean
The Midget
Cucumber (ridge)
Burpee Hybrid
Dwarf Bean
Loch Ness
Lettuce
Little Gem
Marrows, bush
Baby Crookneck, Custard Pie,
Zucchini, Trailing, Little Gem
Peas
Recette
Sweet peppers (capsicum)
Ace F1 Hybrid
Tomatoes
Pixie, Gardeners Delight
Vegetable Bean
Fiskeby V

Herbs for window boxes
Basil
Bergamot
Chives
Parsley
Rosemary
Thymes

Larger herbs for containers
Apple Mint (alone in container to
restrict roots)
Evergreen Bay
Fennel
Lemon Balm
Lovage
Rosemary
Sage
Tarragon
Winter Savory

INDEX

Pictures supplied by:
AFA Colour Library 48; A-Z Collection 41, 42-3 (2 pics), 49; D. Arminson 73br, 79bc; Elly Arnstein/Photo Stephen Sandon 88; P. Ayers 75t; Barnaby's Picture Library 22; P. Becker 99; John Bethell 68b; Steve Bicknell 10, 95; Michael Boys 25tl, 93; M. Chaffer/Design Anthony Wilson 61; P. Chapman 77t; Chevron Chem. Co./Autho. Div. 87; Chilstone 31; R. J. Corbin 6l, 6br, 7tr, 14r, 16, 26r, 27t, 27b, 35l, 36l, 36r, 37tl, 37tr, 37bl, 37br, 65r, 66, 67t, 67b, 75b, 76tc, 78, 86tc, 90l, 90r, 91l, 94tl, 94cr, 100t, 100c, 100b; J. E. Downward 15, 17; Michael Dunne 69tr; Alan Duns 46-7, 52; Dr. Elkan 74t,
79tr; V. Finnis 6tr, 11, 24tl, 29t, 42, 64l, 79bl, 79tl, 83r; B. Furner 2-3, 32, 80, 84-5, 91r; P. Genereux 39, 82; I. Hardwick 23br; R. Heath 81; J. Hovell 64r; P. Hunt 1, 20l, 29b, 51; G. Hyde 50r, 83l; Leslie Johns 14bl, 18, 23tr, 28, 50l, 65bl, 69bc, 81, 94tr; R. Kaye 73tl, 73bl; David Levin 9, 56, 57, 58-9, 60b; Chris Lewis 72; Bill McLaughlin 38 (courtesy Lucy Lambton), 62, 63; Elsa Megson 31b; Nigel Messett 60t; Murphy's 99b; NHPA 98; M. Nimmo 94cl; R. Procter 8r, 13tl, 13tr; Ruth Rutter 19, 20r, 21, 30l, 35r; Kim Sayer 4; Harry Smith 5, 7tl, 7bl, 24bl, 30r, 33, 53, 55, 65tl, 71, 73tr; Peter Stiles 40, 70; Tjaden 74b; Anthony Verlang 68-9; C. Williams 76br, 77b.